Content
MARKETING
MADE EASY

The **Simple, Step-by-Step System** *to* **Attract Your Ideal Audience** & **Put Your Marketing** *on* **Autopilot** *using* **Blogs, Podcasts, Videos, Social Media** & **More!**

John **Nemo**

CW00839853

Content **MARKETING** MADE EASY

Copyright © 2018 Nemo Media Group
Published by John Nemo
St. Paul, Minnesota 55125

All rights reserved. No part of this publication may be reproduced, stored in a retrieval system, or transmitted in any form or by any means—electronic, mechanical, digital, photocopy, recording, or any other—except for brief quotations in printed reviews, without the prior permission of the publisher.

Book cover and interior design by Gregory Rohm

Printed in the United States of America

What Others Say About **John Nemo**

"You know me. I don't recommend people lightly. John Nemo is worth your time. Jump on this!" - *Chris Brogan, New York Times Bestselling Author & Speaker*

"After witnessing John's expertise up close and personal, it's easy to see why he's been crushing it on LinkedIn the past few years. Simply put, when it comes to LinkedIn, John Nemo is the real deal. Can't wait to share more of his LinkedIn knowledge bombs with the rest of Fire Nation soon!" - *John Lee Dumas, Host, Award-Winning "Entrepreneur on Fire" Podcast*

"It's a pleasure to recommend John as both a high-quality human being and a true professional. He invests himself in dramatically improving all aspects of your marketing where he feels he can add value. Overall, an excellent experience and I'm very honored to recommend him." - *Bob Burg, International Bestselling Author of "The Go Giver" & Keynote Speaker*

"I highly encourage you to check out John Nemo. I know it will make a difference for you just like it has for me!" - *Tom Ziglar, CEO, Ziglar, Inc.*

"In this world of so-called, 'online-guru's' who are simply out to make a buck and underdeliver, John Nemo is an incredible find. I have been communicating back and forth with John for over 2 years. And this was before I paid him a single dime to help me build my business. Not only is he extremely knowledgeable, but for me personally, he is an authentic human being. I can think of no better teacher and no better programs than what John is offering with his online courses. Jump on them now and watch your business grow!" - *Lou Rodriguez, P.A., Real Estate Agent*

"Where to begin? A quick look at John's work and it's obvious to see that he's a very detailed-oriented, hardworking, creative, and generous person. I've discovered that the content he gives away for free is just as valuable (if not more so) than the stuff many others have you pay a significant amount for. I'm just getting started with implementing some of his ideas and tips and I'm already seeing progress. Can't wait to see where my business is in six months because of John!" - *Jerry Lopez, Product Support Engineer, Teradata*

"John is an eloquent, effective and, most importantly, an entertaining speaker, teacher and author - not necessarily in this order! He is definitely changing people's lives. What is better than that?" - *Michele M. Palmer, CII, Cachet International, Inc., Global Asset Investigations*

Also by *John Nemo*

FICTION

Miller's Miracle   Jumper   The King's Game

NONFICTION

FiredUp!
*Ignite Your Passion.
Love Your Work.
Live Your Legacy.*

LinkedIn Riches:
*Generate Leads and
Increase Revenue!*

(Mostly)
True Stories:
*47 Essays on the
Laughter of Life*

Share This:
*Labor Unions
and Social Media*

Table of *Contents*

*"Whether your childhood was idyllic or abusive,
the challenge stands: Do you accept yourself
as one utterly loved by God?"*

- Brennan Manning

Here's a photo of me around age 4 or 5

Dedication

I often tear up when I see photos of myself as a small boy.

The tears are from the unhealed, broken places inside me that those images remind me of. Of abuse suffered by a little boy who is now 43 years old.

If you were abused growing up, it can be *really* hard to trust, and *really* hard to let love in. I struggle so much with self-hatred and depression sometimes.

But I trust in Jesus Christ. I trust in His healing, His love and His acceptance.

(Not religion. Just Jesus.)

I know this is a book about Content Marketing, but the *content* of my life is the story I've lived so far.

And I've come to believe that my story (and yours, if you choose) will have a happy ending.

One where every tear is wiped away and every wrong is made right. One where joy replaces suffering, and love replaces pain.

Where reunions are joyous, laughs are boisterous and love is at the center of it all.

I believe all of this to be true because I believe Jesus Christ is who He says He is - the greatest Hero and Savior who ever lived.

Jesus is the Hero of my story and my life, and I am forever grateful that he rescued me and saved me, and that I'm loved as I am, not as I should be ... because nobody is as they should be, to paraphrase Brennan Manning.

"Each day, proclaim the good news that [Jesus] saves. Publish his glorious deeds among the nations." - Psalms 96:2-3

Chapter 1:

Step Zero - What is Content Marketing and How Does it Work?

The pavement pushed back against my frantic feet, sending shockwaves through my aching shins and caring little that I was lost, late and panicked.

I raced along the downtown sidewalk, frantically scanning for signs of my destination as I bumped into pedestrians and tripped over curbs.

A police officer standing on a corner eyed me with suspicion as I huffed toward him.

"Excuse me," I asked, gulping for breath. "Do you know where the Target Center Arena is?"

It was 1992, and I was 16 years old.

I was about to discover an incredible secret, one that would prove to be a catalyst for every ounce of success I've ever achieved.

At that moment, however, I simply felt like a fool.

Urban Cowboy that I was, I couldn't find the Target Center, an enormous sports arena located in the heart of downtown Minneapolis, Minnesota.

The police officer pointed me in the right direction, and I raced several more blocks to the stadium, where the NBA's Minnesota Timberwolves were holding a special sportswriting clinic for aspiring high school journalists.

Late, sweaty and out of breath, I attended the clinic, which culminated with a special writing contest put on by the Minnesota High School Newspaper Association.

After touring the arena and locker rooms, meeting with local sportswriters and learning about how they covered the team and the challenges of the job, we were all asked to write a story about the event and what we learned.

It was a big deal: The winning writer would have his or her work featured as the cover story in an issue of *Timberwolves Tonight Magazine,* along with getting free tickets to a few games and other honors.

After the event ended, I found a payphone (remember, it was 1992) and called my father at home.

"Uh, dad, I can't remember where I parked the car downtown," I told him. "Can you pick me up outside Target Center?"

He did, and we spent the next hour or so driving in and out of parking ramps around downtown Minneapolis, looking for the car I'd parked in a panic before tearing through the city streets looking for the Target Center.

The next day, I sat down to write my story.

Here's how I started it:

As an aspiring journalist, I have often heard that the life of a beat writer can be a tough one.

My suspicions were not confirmed, however, until the day of the Minnesota Timberwolves sportswriting clinic. That day, I found myself lost in downtown Minneapolis, unable to find the enormous Target Center.

I knew then that my life as a prospective sportswriter was not starting out too well. Luckily, I found a police officer, and after I told him my plight, he somewhat amusedly pointed me in the right direction.

After about eight blocks at top speed, I panted into the Target Center, just in time to begin the clinic. Just as abruptly as my unscheduled tour of Minneapolis ended, my other tour began.

This was to be a journey into the life of sportswriters, and how they went about covering an NBA team.

I went on in the article to describe what I learned at the clinic, and then finished my story with this:

Most days for a sportswriter are pretty similar, and one of the most important parts of covering a team is establishing and maintaining an open relationship between the two sides.

But in my opinion, the most important thing sportswriters need to know when covering an NBA team is this: They need to be able to find the arena on their own, instead of following their father's directions.

A few weeks later, I got a phone call from the Timberwolves - I'd won the contest!

My father forgot all about my parking woes (and cheap shots about his skill in providing driving directions) and proudly took me to the first of several games we got free tickets to.

As we walked into the Target Center, my father spotted a vendor hawking copies of that evening's *Timberwolves Tonight Magazine.*

I still have the issue:

My story was on the cover, and my dad broke into a huge smile.

"Hey buddy, wanna buy your kid a program?" the vendor asked my dad as we approached.

"Indeed I do!" my dad told the vendor. "In fact, my son wrote the article that's featured on the cover!"

The vendor looked over at me.

"No kidding?" he said. "That's great, kid."

He turned back to my dad.

"That'll be five bucks, buddy."

The Magic of Content Marketing and "Infotainment"

As we sat in our seats that night and watched the game, I realized that *content* was the reason I was sitting inside an NBA arena for free.

Content was the reason my dad was telling everyone who had a game program, "Hey! My son wrote the article you're reading!"

Content was why I was the envy of all my high school buddies.

Even more important (and even as a 16 year old) I *knew* the reason I won was because of how I'd put my *personality* into my content.

In later years, I'd come up with a term to capture what I'd discovered: *Infotainment.*

People want information, yes, but they *also* want to be entertained while consuming that information.

Information + Entertainment = Infotainment.

That evening in 1992, I understood clearly that creating unique and original content which entertained, inspired and educated others was something that would open doors for me.

Today, more than 25 years later, I sit atop a career built on content - from writing 8 books to thousands of newspaper and magazine stories to hundreds of press releases, blog posts, talk radio segments, podcasts, videos and webinars.

Content = Currency

And what was true in 1992 is even more true today: You must *earn* the time, attention and interest of others you want to engage with and/or sell your products and services to.

And the way you *earn* that time, interest and attention is through the unique, valuable and entertaining *content* you create and share.

This is what content marketing is all about and why it matters so much.

In today's marketplace, content has become the currency you use to "buy" the time, attention and interest of audiences you want to sell your products and services to.

Gone are the days of just *asking* someone for time on the phone or in person to consider what you can offer.

Instead, you must "purchase" a prospect's time and attention *first* through the content you create.

Best of all, once you've proven and demonstrated your authority and expertise through your content (a blog post, a book, a podcast, a video, etc.) people are eager to talk to you and do business with you.

Why I Gave a Guy in Tennessee My Money and Hope

I once sat through an hour-long business meeting about fake trees and men in tights.

I remember looking around the conference room, seeing a cloudless blue sky and sunshine through the window, freedom just beyond my grasp.

Inside, my colleagues discussed in passionate tones what type of fake foliage to order for a "Robin Hood" themed protest, and whether or not a troupe of male actors in tights, masks and pointy hats should be brought in to illustrate the benefits of the "Robin Hood Tax" our organization was being mandated to support.

I was sitting inside that conference room as an employee who (thanks to the benefits of my labor union contract) was guaranteed a 6 percent raise each year regardless of performance. I was making an unreal salary, had incredible health benefits, and was about to qualify for a defined-benefit retirement pension (which are all but extinct in today's corporate environment).

To top it off, I knew that short of standing on the roof of our building with a bullhorn and shouting that I was anti-union, it was all but impossible to get fired thanks to our contract.

(Note: This isn't meant to be an anti-union screed. I'm just stating the reality of my employment situation at the time.)

I had it made. It was a cake job, one I could coast through for the next 20-30 years, piling up my pension and benefits without the pressure to perform or the fear of being fired without warning.

I couldn't wait to quit.

As my colleagues talked about the importance of plastic trees and colored tights in the fight against the nation's wealthy elite, I looked out the window and thought to myself: *"Is this really all there is? Is this really what my life has become?"*

I quit the job a few months later, leaving behind the career version of a "sure thing" and instead launching my own marketing agency without any real savings, clients or assurances I'd make it.

Before quitting, I'd read a book that convinced me my instincts about marketing were correct, and that I *could* make my own agency work.

Consuming the *content* of this book, *Brand Against The Machine* by John Michael Morgan, not only fired me up and convinced me to quit my day job... it also made me want to give the author (John Morgan) more of my time, attention and money.

After reading the *content* John shared inside his book - content that was infused with his personality (in particular a sarcastic sense of humor and laugh-out-loud funny jokes about his mother-in-law) I knew that not only had I come to *know* and *like* John Michael Morgan, but that I could *trust* him to help me with my new business venture.

As soon as I finished the book, I contacted John online and told him I wanted to buy an hour of his 1-on-1 consulting time.

John didn't need to sell me on his expertise or convince me to pay him his hourly rate for coaching calls.

His *content* had already done the heavy lifting.

Six years later, I *still* pay John each and every month to coach me in my business, and here I am promoting him and his coaching program to countless others in my own book!

That is the power of content marketing.

Gone Fishin' - Content Marketing Explained

Allow me one more illustration to really drive home the importance of using content in your marketing efforts.

Here in the United States, I live in Minnesota, known as the "Land of 10,000 Lakes."

As you can imagine, people here are bonkers about fishing.

However, when you go fishing, you don't just walk up to a lake and yell into the water, "Excuse me! Mr. Fish? I'd love to have a few minutes of your time to discuss possible synergies between you leaving your natural habitat and me cooking you up for dinner. What do you say?"

After all, you can't just *ask* a fish to jump into your boat.

Instead, you have to bring a fishing pole and (most important) *bait* with you.

And, the more tantalizing your bait is, the more likely you are to catch a prospective fish as a result.

So, when it comes to Content Marketing, your *content* (be it a blog post, a book, a webinar, a video, etc.) is the *bait.*

Your ideal *prospects* are the *fish.*

And, just like with fishing, the type of "bait" you use with Content Marketing determines the type of prospect you'll catch the attention of.

For example, if you want some quick bites from smaller fish, you can easily throw a worm onto a hook (think of a short blog post or video).

If you want to catch a whale, you'll need to put in more time and effort, producing a larger, more tantalizing piece of bait (think of a webinar, a book, etc.) that will attract the biggest fish in the ocean.

A Personal Matter

Let's leave the ocean for a moment and get back to what great content encompasses.

Because it's *not* just enough to create a piece of content that solves a problem or shares helpful advice or tips.

Where content *really* becomes powerful is when you imbue it with your unique personality and communication style.

When you sprinkle your own personality and style of communicating into your original content, you attract an audience who will get to know, like and (most important!) remember you as a person.

Now, you'll also repel some people as part of the process, but that's fine - do you really want to work with people who don't appreciate or enjoy your personality and communication style?

As anyone in any sort of business environment knows, people like to do business with someone they *know, like* and *trust.*

If the content you create is devoid of all personality and "just the facts," you might create *trust* with your intended audience, but they won't *know or like* you, and that makes it much harder to get their business.

Worst of all, if your content lacks personality, people will *forget you* - and there is no bigger challenge in today's always-on, nonstop online marketplace then being ignored or forgotten!

Instead, when you insert your personality into your content, sharing stories and allowing people to get to know and like you, something indispensable happens: People now have a *narrative* to attach to you.

This is critical, because the way our brains work is through *story.* When you tell someone a compelling story about who you are and what you do, *and* you tell that story as part of a compelling piece of content, people will *remember you.*

Maybe you're the stay-at-home mom who turned her passion for crafts into a successful online business using Etsy. (And now you teach other stay-at-home moms how to do it.)

Maybe you're the former veteran who served in the U.S. Army and now has a passion for helping other military personnel transition into the workplace.

In either case, people now have a "hook" or "story" they can remember you by. Especially if you've included images of you playing with your kids (stay-at-home mom) or wearing a uniform from your days in the military (veteran).

How It Looks

When I share my story via a webinar, podcast or other content, I have a very specific *narrative* I use: Born the son of two English professors, I grew up in a home where the basement was literally lined from floor to ceiling with books.

I talk about how that upbringing led me into a love of story, and later a career telling and selling stories via journalism and public relations.

And then, how, trapped in a job I wasn't passionate about (remember the story about the meeting on fake trees and Robin Hood tights?), I took a giant risk and quit my "safe" day job to start my own business, working from home and spending more time with my wife and our three wild young boys.

As I was writing this chapter, I actually was interrupted with a phone call from a customer.

"You know, the reason I signed up for your LinkedIn lead generation training program was your personality that you always share in your content," she told me. "I knew you were someone who I'd enjoy learning from, that you saw life the same way I did."

Talk about proof of concept!

Want To Sell More? Get Emotional!

Remember, this is a book about sales and marketing.

As human beings, we make *emotional, impulsive decisions* to buy a product or service.

Later on, yes, we utilize *logic* to justify our purchase, but people buy based on emotion.

For example, I hired John Morgan as my business coach because, after reading his book, I *liked* him. I felt too like I *knew* John - that he would be someone who I'd get along with well.

I was able to *justify* the time and money spent with John because of the knowledge and information he shared with me, but what caused me to do business with him was the *emotional affinity* his content created for me as a reader.

Here's a quick story to illustrate this concept of *emotional vs. practical* behavior when it comes to buying products and services.

The Time I Spent $35,000 To Feel Emasculated

I never felt like less of a man than I did in that moment.

I was the "proud" new owner of a minivan.

In reality, I'd just spent $35,000 to discard any remaining vestiges of my manhood.

After all, what I *really* wanted was a gigantic, gas-guzzling, completely *impractical* SUV.

The reason was simple: When I drove that monstrosity down the road, I *felt* like a man again.

One small problem: The SUV cost $65,000.

In reality, the minivan was far more *practical* and a much better fit for what our young family needed at the time. Even more, it cost $30,000 less than the SUV and the gas mileage was twice as good.

And yet, I've never been more miserable making a purchase in my life.

Therein lies the lesson of this story: *We buy based on emotion.*

"People buy the way the process makes them *feel*," Bestselling Author Seth Godin notes.

We later go back and justify our purchase with facts, figures and stats, but we *never* buy because of those things. We might tell ourselves we do, but in reality, we're using those stats and figures to make ourselves feel like we're getting an amazing deal.

Your Content Must Make People *Feel* Something

If, like me, you sell products or services online for a living, you must make someone *feel* something as part of the process when it comes to the content you create and share.

Back to the minivan for a minute.

The lesson was driven (no pun intended) home the other night when a good buddy of mine, Mark Ehling, came over to jam on guitars.

Back in our early 20s, Mark and I would get together and jam for hours.

The other night, Mark pulled up to my house ... in a bright green minivan.

With two young boys of his own, a minivan is the "practical" and "smart" purchase for Mark as well.

However, I knew that making that purchase was not a *feeling* he enjoyed.

The Foundation is Laid - Ready to Start?

So far I've covered what Content Marketing truly "is" and why it matters so much to the success of your business in today's marketplace.

In the chapters to come, we're going to dive deeper into specific strategies, tactics and techniques that ensure you're able to create the type of content that makes your marketing efforts irresistible.

Let's go!

Chapter 2:
Seamless Selling - Content That Converts

If, like me, you were fortunate enough to be born in the 1970s (or earlier), you remember a world when the Internet didn't dominate everything we do.

You also remember dressing like this during the late 1980s and early 1990s:

That's me in the middle, complete with rolled jeans and deck shoes. I'm flanked on each side by my older sisters - Clare demonstrating the spiked bangs hairstyle and Jennifer the leather bomber jacket fashion made so popular thanks to Tom Cruise and *Top Gun*.

Now, my point in both embarrassing myself and my sisters (never going to miss a chance to do that) is simple: The world (and the way we create and share content) has moved on.

Allow me to explain.

Back in the early 1990s, the Internet was just something Al Gore was still thinking of inventing.

(Yes, I know Al Gore didn't invent the internet. Please don't email me. As we become better friends, my sarcasm and sense of humor will become more apparent.)

Today, easy access to the Internet and the advent of the iPhone means you can literally consume content in any form you like (written, audio, still images or video) anywhere and anytime you like.

When I was growing up in Minneapolis-St. Paul during the 1980s, we had all of five TV channels to choose from - the three big networks (ABC, CBS and NBC) and two UHF channels.

Unlike the "rich" people who had cable TV, my parents (both English professors) told me to go read a book instead of begging them for cable every day.

Here's what was *really* crazy about the pre-Internet era from a professional and content marketing standpoint: If I wanted to publish a written piece of content and have it read by a large audience, I had to either get hired by a newspaper or magazine, secure a book publishing deal or spend insane amounts of money to purchase advertising in written periodicals.

Also, if I wanted people around the city (let alone the world) to hear my voice, I had to work at a talk radio station or (again) pay the gatekeepers of those radio stations for access to their audiences via advertising.

Finally, if I wanted to record a video, I'd need several hundred dollars (and that was a lot of money in the 1980s) to purchase a clunky video camera, let alone a microphone or other equipment. If I wanted to edit my video, I'd need to break into a local TV news station and utilize one of their editing suites.

If I wanted anyone to actually *see* my video, I'd (again) have to pay to have a television network or station run my content, or else get hired as a TV news reporter or camera person.

Do you see what I'm getting at here?

Things are far easier and more cost-effective today when it comes to creating and distributing content to a worldwide audience.

Today, you have *zero* gatekeepers telling you what type of content you can create or share.

(That's the only explanation for why my teenage sons think it's "fun" to watch YouTube videos of other kids playing video games and commenting on their performance. Or why Psy's video for *Gangnam Style* has 66 million views online and spawned the worst earworm in music history.)

This is more important than you think, because the lack of gatekeepers (think, editors) curating or controlling the type of content you create and limiting the audiences you share it with means you can be as unique and original as you please.

For instance, there is a 6 year old who makes $11 million a year playing with toys and posting the videos on YouTube.

(You can read the story here - http://bit.ly/2tG5Ps3)

You might think it's ridiculous, but it doesn't matter, because the *marketplace* now determines what is considered "good" content.

YouTube views have replaced the approval of film and television critics.

Pageviews on blog posts have usurped legions of literary critics.

Podcast downloads have rendered talk radio station managers and program directors moot.

Today, if you have an iPhone and a data connection, you can stream video of yourself live to a worldwide audience on Facebook or countless other platforms in real time.

The World Has Changed

If you grew up, as I did, during the pre-Internet era of mass communication methods, you realize the seismic shift we've undergone when it comes to our ability to create and communicate with each other.

Or, if you're one of those lazy millennials (again, kidding!), I cannot state this with enough emphasis: *We are living through the biggest and most radical change in how human beings communicate since the invention of the printing press.*

Actually, this is more like the invention of the printing press, radio and television all rolled into one. It's that massive and that life-changing.

All this is great news, because it means content is easier (and more affordable) than ever to create.

However, it also means that the "quality" and "value" of content has become completely subjective.

For instance, my boys think watching YouTube videos of a random teeanger screaming into the microphone while playing *Madden* on his Xbox is a cinematic masterpiece.

I'd rather have my fingernails pulled out one by one than watch those videos, but my opinion matters not. For this target audience of teenage, video-game crazed boys, *that* type of content is what the marketplace rewards right now.

The same is true in business - *you* get to create your own unique, original content, and *you* get to decide what target audiences you want it to appeal to.

And, once you put it out there, the *marketplace* will make it abundantly clear if people love it or hate it.

Content That Converts

Now, rather than having to guess at what goes into creating great content that results in people wanting to do business with you, there are some proven strategies and techniques you can utilize to ensure your content works.

People, after all, have not changed.

Technology has, of course, but the type of content people respond to has not.

People cannot help but consume, share and engage with content that is ...

Humorous.

Enthusiastic.

Shocking.

Unexpected.

Emotional.

Inspiring.

Feeding Starving Children

I once spent an afternoon inside an enormous field house, packing freeze-dried meals for starving children in Africa.

After our shift was done, we sat down for a presentation on the problem of world hunger. The statistics didn't seem real, and even felt numbing - it was impossible to imagine millions of kids really not having enough food to eat or clean water to drink every single day of their lives.

Then the presenter shared a video.

A few minutes later, I was weeping and opening my wallet to donate more money than I've ever given to any single cause.

In the video, we met some of the children that this organization (<u>Feed My Starving Children</u>) helped.

The *emotion* that the video content evoked (seeing these kids, once starving and living in abject poverty, now happy, smiling and having a basic life need met) was undeniable.

It was *shocking* to see real people, real children, suffering this way.

It was also *inspiring* to see how volunteers *just like me* were making a difference in their lives by providing safe and nutritious meals through this organization.

That video moved me in a way statistics and data could not.

Seeing the children in the video, I was *inspired* to do more than just pack a few meals.

The video's content made me *emotional,* and ready to take action.

Right as the video ended and the lights came up, I wiped tears from my eyes. I heard sniffles and sighs from the audience.

The presenter explained how, in addition to the volunteering we'd just done, donating money to the organization would help even more children just like the ones we'd met in the video.

Without hesitation, I pulled out my credit card to donate. I did it while I was still *emotional* - feeling inspired and moved to help a fellow human being in need.

That is the power of content marketing done right.

Easier Than Ever

Here's some more good news: Telling a compelling story using creative content has never been easier (or more valuable) than it is right now.

And, unlike the rolled jeans, spiked bangs heyday of the late 1980's and early 1990's that I came of age in, we don't need a printing press or TV station to create and distribute it.

Thanks to technology, *everyone is now a media outlet,* armed with the ability to instantly share audio, video or written content anytime (and from anywhere!) with a worldwide audience.

Seamless Selling - Why Content Works So Well

To this point, I've explored and explained why content is now so ubiquitous thanks to the technological era we live in.

I've also demonstrated that there are certain timeless concepts and principles packed inside of great content that transcend the era or platform used to share certain stories and messages.

Next, let's explore why content is so effective in selling your products and services - especially online, and especially with a "cold" audience who has never heard of you prior to consuming your content.

Screen Time = Sales Time

According to the Kaiser Family Foundation, kids ages 8-18 now spend 7.5 hours every single day in front of screens consuming content for entertainment purposes.

Another study revealed that the average adult spends more than 9 hours per day in front of a screen for work and/or entertainment purposes. A Huffington Post article cited research where people are checking their iPhone 85 times a day to consume content.

Think about your own life. How many hours a day do you spend in front of a screen of some sort? In the evening, do you watch TV *while* you have your iPhone in your hand, scrolling through your Facebook or Twitter feeds during commercial breaks? Do you pop in your earbuds and listen to a Podcast while walking the dog or mowing the lawn?

Ignoring the debate about whether or not all this screen time is good for us, let's look at this from a business perspective - if we want to be in front of our ideal clients and customers online, we better be putting out content!

Content has never been easier to consume, and our society continues to move away from *interruption-based* engagement (think cold calls, door-to-door sales, television commercials, etc.) and into *self-selection* (choosing who to follow on social networks or using search engines to find content online) and *passive engagement* (reading blog posts, listening to podcasts, etc.)

Your customer now *chooses* and self-selects what he or she wants to read, watch or listen to. Also, he or she chooses *when* to consume it.

Content = Currency

These days, you cannot simply interrupt someone to ask for his or her time or attention, let alone money. Instead, you must *earn* that right through the content you create.

Think about it. Especially if someone has never heard of you before, why would he or she give you the most valuable commodity on earth ... his or her time?

So, assuming you want to "buy" the time, attention and interest of your ideal prospects online, you must create content that will be of intense interest (and value) to them.

Creating and sharing free, valuable content that helps a niche audience solve some of their biggest professional problems is how you set yourself apart from the competition.

This is the key. When you solve a problem for someone or help him or her get a quick win, he or she immediately begins to *Know, Like* and *Trust* you.

Especially when you're entering into a relationship with a new, "cold" prospect online, you must start by helping them solve a problem or meet a need. And you must do it on *their* terms, without asking for their personal time, attention or any other type of commitment.

Below is an example of a how guy wearing a popcorn bucket on his head (yours truly) got internationally-recognized keynote speakers, *New York Times* Bestselling Authors and other A-List business owners and entrepreneurs to endorse him online.

How To Get Famous People To Endorse You

As evidenced by the image below, I'm just another guy wearing a plastic popcorn bucket on his head while playing "Star Wars" with my boys at home:

My point: I'm just a regular guy, a virtual nobody.

And yet, I've been able to get *New York Times* Bestselling Authors, internationally known business icons and other "big shots" to promote my LinkedIn online course and trainings to their massive audiences.

The list includes, among others: Mari Smith, Tom Ziglar (son of Zig Ziglar), Chris Brogan, Bob Burg, John Lee Dumas, Ray Edwards and Jairek Robbins (son of Tony Robbins).

And, I'll spend the next few paragraphs demonstrating how you can do the exact same thing – even if you're a virtual "nobody" like me.

The first – and most important – step in this process is understanding how to go about contacting your ideal "big shots" in the first place.

In every instance, I've found LinkedIn to be the most effective method.

Here's why: LinkedIn has killed the gatekeepers.

When you send someone a direct, 1-on-1 message on LinkedIn, not only does the person see it in his or her LinkedIn inbox, but he or she also might get an alert on his or her phone (if they have it enabled) along with getting an email sent to his or her primary email address.

(Almost everyone who originally set up a LinkedIn account, even years ago, used his or her primary email address. This is key!)

With that in mind, you can get busy connecting to your "big shot" on LinkedIn.

First, send a personalized invitation to the "big shot" inviting him or her to connect on LinkedIn. With the text of your invitation, treat the big shot like a normal person. Don't fawn and gush over him or her. Instead, acknowledge what you like about his or her work, why he or she will want to connect with you and why you're reaching out. Save the hype and hyperbole – be straightforward, friendly and professional in tone.

If the "big shot" doesn't allow random connections (meaning you have to have his or her personal email to send a LinkedIn invite), use a LinkedIn InMail to send a direct note.

Either way, LinkedIn affords you several methods to reach your "big shot" directly.

In my case, I reached out to a handful of "big shots" on LinkedIn, and almost all of them mentioned in their replies to me that they noticed my message personally.

Many then handed me off to an assistant or employee to work on the details of our new relationship, but my point is this: They engaged with me! I had the start of a relationship to build from.

Once you're connected, you have to quickly demonstrate how you can help this "big shot" in a way where he or she not only takes notice of you, but also wants to reply as quickly as possible. You'll want to be creative, credible and quick.

One of the A-List business celebrities who has given me permission to talk at length about our relationship is Chris Brogan.

Chris is a *New York Times* and *Wall Street Journal* International Bestselling Author, Speaker and Consultant who works with clients including Google, Disney, IBM, Microsoft and many more.

To paraphrase Will Ferrell's character from *Anchorman*, Chris Brogan is "kind of a big deal."

He's also humble, genuine, self-deprecating and one of the nicer human beings on the planet.

I approached Chris cold on LinkedIn and told him that I wanted to rewrite his entire LinkedIn profile for free. I also explained that he didn't have to invest any time or effort in the endeavor.

Instead, I'd take all the risk – I just wanted his permission to try.

I told Chris I'd send him a Microsoft Word document with my suggested changes, along with additional tips on how to improve his LinkedIn profile. He could take what he liked and leave the rest. Or just ignore it completely.

In short, I was taking all the risk and asking nothing of Chris Brogan.

This is important! Too many of us are out there with our virtual hand out, asking for free advice, asking for someone to promote us, asking for someone to buy from us ... and we're doing it without first *earning* the right to make that type of ask.

I knew that with someone like Chris Brogan, I had to earn the right to ask for anything.

So I started with a creative, credible and quick invitation to do something I thought he'd find valuable (rewrite his LinkedIn profile).

Next, I needed to earn his respect and additional attention by actually delivering what I promised – a great LinkedIn profile rewrite.

What I found interesting in reaching out to Chris and other influencers at his level was that *nobody else* had offered this type of service to them.

"I'm going to take you up on your offer, John," one of the other "big shots" told me in a message. "It's funny, because I know a ton of LinkedIn 'experts' who are good friends, but none of them have ever offered to actually rewrite my profile for me. So, sure, go for it!"

Now, this is important: When you get the permission to do someone like Chris Brogan a free favor, you do it like they are paying you top dollar!

I spent hours researching Chris' brand and backstory, doing my best to get into his professional and personal head so that I could create a revamped LinkedIn profile that was both authentic to who he was and helpful to his business goals.

I did the same with the other "big shots" I approached.

Remember: *If you want to get someone's attention, do great work. Dazzle them! Impress them!*

If you do, people feel socially and professionally *obligated* to return the favor and help you out in return.

It's proven that when we give someone something for free, and without (initially) asking for anything in return, the law of reciprocity works its magic. The bigger the favor you do, the more obligated the person feels to pay you back.

After I'd earned Chris' attention and proven my worth by delivering a killer profile rewrite, I made a couple of key "asks" when the time felt right.

The first was to ask Chris to share word about my free LinkedIn training webinars with his audience, which he did in a very generous way via his email list and social media channels.

The second was to ask him for a public testimonial, which he did for me via both video and text.

The third was to ask if I could drop his name in approaching other "big shots," and he again agreed.

It was much easier to land additional "big shots" once I could say, "Hey, I've worked with Chris Brogan, you can ask him all about me. He trusts my work and will vouch for me."

Happy Endings? Not Always

In addition to working with Chris, I've reached out to dozens of other "big shots," and I've rewritten dozens of LinkedIn profiles that took countless hours. All without getting paid a dime.

In some cases – like with Chris – my efforts resulted in huge, game-changing wins for me and my business.

As one of Brogan's followers mentioned to me in a note after Chris promoted me to his tribe, *"John, congrats on the anointing!"*

Despite putting in the same type and quality of work with several other "big shots," results weren't always so grand. But that's okay. I learned a lot about what people at the "A-List" level are like in the business world – what makes them tick, what to watch out for, and much more.

And while some "big shots" didn't want me to publicly mention I rewrote their profiles, they did agree to serve as a private reference when I approach other "A-List" types in their area of the business world.

Like anything, every single attempt doesn't always result in a home run. But I learned something in each instance, and improved the next time out.

In researching the stories behind so many of today's biggest business authors and influencers, I've also seen a common trend: They all started small and worked their faces off to get where they are today. Nobody handed these guys anything.

Why should you expect your journey to be any different?

One final thought – you only have so many hours in a given day. Swing for the fences with your life and business! Reach out to the influencers in your profession, and follow the blueprint I've outlined in this section. Whatever it is you do, you have something of value you can bring to others, no matter how popular or famous they are.

Figure out what that is, and then deliver it without asking for anything in return. Then, once you've built a relationship and demonstrated your value, figure out some "win-win" type "asks" you can make of those celebrities.

Once you do, it can change your professional – and personal – fortunes forever.

Big Wins vs. Small Wins

Now, the story above is a "high risk, high reward" type endeavor using content (in this case, my LinkedIn profile writing skills).

It doesn't always have to be done on such a large or grand scale.

In fact, here's a simple (and fast) way to take that same type of "value first" content marketing approach when connecting with an individual prospect online using a platform like LinkedIn.

Leveraging LinkedIn for Leads

Say, as one example, I want to sell my online course (LinkedIn Riches) to a Business Coach I come across on LinkedIn. First, I'll send that coach a personalized invitation to connect.

Once we've connected, I don't *immediately* ask the coach to attend one of my sales webinars, jump on the phone or anything else.

Instead, I break the ice with some small talk, asking questions about the person's background and Coaching business. (Note: LinkedIn makes this easy to do, because you can see right away on someone's profile where he or she lives, works, went to college, etc. . . . all of which are great icebreakers and conversation starters.)

I also offer the Business Coach a free piece of content that promises a fast, easy and "quick win" for him or her as it relates to utilizing LinkedIn to find new clients.

It's a simple PDF that has a copy-and-paste template you can use to instantly improve your LinkedIn profile.

Once I've connected with and conversed a bit with a Business Coach on LinkedIn to break the ice, I offer up this free template.

I do it by first asking a question ("Curious - are you looking to use LinkedIn at all to find new clients?") and then making an offer ("If you are, I've got a great copy-and-paste template I can give you to help make your profile more client-facing …").

Most important, as part of this script, I've found that I must first *ask permission* ("Would you like a free copy of this template?") before I send the Business Coach a link to my landing page.

If the Coach says "Yes" to my question and offer of some free content, then I reply with a link to a page on my website where he or she can exchange his or her email in order to access the template:

The Ultimate LinkedIn Profile Template
FREE DOWNLOAD!

SEND ME THE TEMPLATE!

What You'll Discover

Get the EXACT words, phrases and formatting hacks that turn your LinkedIn Profile Summary into a lead-generating, client-attracting piece of content.

It's "copy-and-paste" simple and takes just a few minutes to apply!

The Business Coach just has to enter his or her email to get access to the template. Once that happens, I can now deliver even *more* helpful content via an email autoresponder sequence.

In this example, I've set up the email autoresponder to first deliver the free template, and then, over time, share more free content *specific* to Business Coaches and how they can achieve one of their goals (finding new clients on LinkedIn).

Eventually, I'll invite those Business Coaches to attend a free training webinar that shares additional free content and then finishes with an offer to join my paid training program for a special price and bonus package.

All of this is done on *the other person's schedule,* from the time they opt-in to get the template to when they open my emails to when they decide to attend my automated webinar.

Using content marketing this way saves you immense time and helps pre-qualify your best prospects. By warming up a Business Coach *first* with some "quick win" content (the profile template PDF, some blog posts and short training videos, etc.), by the time they attend my sales webinar, they already know, like and trust me and have seen some tangible results from my strategies.

Remember: The more someone self-selects to consume the additional free content you offer, the deeper he or she moves into your sales funnel.

And, like starting with free samples of your homemade chocolate chip cookies before selling a hungry customer an entire box, your free content takes people on a journey that helps them get to Know, Like and Trust you *before* they're ever given an opportunity to buy something.

Don't Claim. Demonstrate.

Here's another important reason you need to create and share free content with prospects online that demonstrates your expertise.

In today's online world, anyone can *claim* authority. In fact, it seems like everywhere you turn, you see another person calling himself or herself a "guru," "ninja" or whatever else.

To really win someone's trust, you must *demonstrate* authority. Your free content *proves* to people that you are the expert, that you can help them achieve their goals and that you are worth their time, interest and attention.

Going back to the previous example, if you're a Business Coach I just met on LinkedIn, I can *tell* you how great I am at helping others win new business on the platform.

Or, I can *show* you I know what I'm doing by giving you a piece of content that is fast, free and easy to implement. And, once you see I'm the real deal, that my tips actually work and help you get a quick win, you're much more likely to want to hear more of what I have to say, right?

Your Ask = Amount of Trust Earned.

Keep this in mind: The bigger your "ask" of someone, the more trust you must earn.

After all, you don't ask someone to marry you on the first date, and you can't ask someone for a sale as soon as you get connected and exchange a few pleasantries on a platform like LinkedIn.

Instead, your "ask" must always be in direct proportion to the amount of trust you've earned with the other person up to that point in the relationship.

The bigger your ask, the more trust you need to earn before you make it. As a result, the quality and value of the free content you share must reflect that reality.

The Riches are in the Niches

Here's another important lesson: Whenever possible, your content should be hyper-focused on a targeted, niche audience, to the point of including their job title or industry name in the headline of your blog posts and articles.

Say, for example, that you want to sell video marketing services. And that one of your target markets is chiropractors.

Using a professional platform like LinkedIn, you can instantly and easily find countless chiropractors to connect with and market your services to.

And, just like anyone else, those chiropractors will want to feel like you really "get" their industry and all the unique challenges and issues they face on a daily basis.

So, while you *can* do video marketing for anyone, you want to make sure that on LinkedIn, at least, you make it clear that you specialize in helping *chiropractors* use online video to get new patients. Your content should reflect this strategy.

For instance, you can publish a blog post titled, "3 Ways Chiropractors Can Leverage Video To Land New Patients."

This post might be the same tips you'd give *anyone* in any sort of business who wants to use video marketing, but that small and subtle tweak (including chiropractors in the headline and using *their* language of "patients" instead of "customers") makes all the difference.

Here's how the post could look: You start off with an introduction about the explosion of video online - how YouTube has become the world's second largest search engine, how Google now *owns* YouTube and thus integrates those videos into search results, and so on.

Then, you can point out as your first tip the importance of online video for Search Engine Optimization (SEO) and getting "found" online via sites like Google and Bing.

Second, you could point out how video helps *humanize* you as a Chiropractor - people get to see your office, "meet" you via video, see your face, hear your voice, respond to your smile and personality, etc. You can then share how a chiropractor can talk about understanding the importance of a patient feeling comfortable with his or her provider given how personal and intimate the service is, and how this can come across well on a video, etc.

Third, you could talk about how video can be used to showcase your services, having clients share testimonials on camera about how great you are, about a specific injury or pain your chiropractic services helped alleviate, and so on. Explain how this helps prospective patients feel right at home, because they'll be able to relate to the people in your video and might even have some of the same issues or injuries.

Inside the blog post, you can insert some your own marketing videos that you've previously done for chiropractors, helping demonstrate or show the different tips at work.

Finally, finish with a call to action inviting your reader (chiropractors and their office managers) to reach out and connect with you directly to discuss how *they* can get started with online videos today.

See how this piece of content unfolded? You started with a niche-specific headline (Chiropractors), promised to help them meet a need they have (get more patients), and then shared some practical reasons and tips of why video will help them achieve this goal.

Finally, you demonstrated *your* expertise and authority through the video samples and content, and finished with an opportunity for the reader to go further by connecting with you directly.

Headlines = Heroic Content

Now, you can create the greatest piece of content in the world, but if the headline is confusing, boring or uninspiring, nobody will consume it!

My favorite headline formula for blog posts and other pieces of content is as follows: "Target Audience Name + Your Service + Benefit They Want".

Let's break down the Chiropractor example.

Here's the headline:

"3 Ways Chiropractors Can Leverage Video To Land New Patients!"

Chiropractor = Target Audience

Video = Your Service

New Patients = Benefit They Want

See how simple this is? When you start creating content that helps a specific, niche audience solve *their* biggest problems or meet *their* biggest goals, you're well on your way to selling your products and services on the other side.

(Note: For more headline tips and ideas, grab a free copy of my "Headline Hero" ebook. You can get it at https://linkedinriches.com/hh-checkout/)

Chapter 3:
Idea Factory - How To Come Up With Content Your Audience Will Go Bananas For

Before you set out to create a piece of content, you need to have a plan.

You don't try and build a house without a blueprint, and you shouldn't start crafting content without an end in mind. Also, if you want to create content that helps sell your products and services, you have to figure out *who* you want engaging with it.

As I say inside my *LinkedIn Riches* Book and Online Course, the riches are in the niches in today's online marketplace. Meaning the more you try and create content that is everything to everyone, the faster you will fail.

Instead, you must focus on a specific, niche audience, and craft content that appeals to them on multiple levels - emotional, practical and so on.

Finding Your Audience

The biggest mistake I made when I started my own business online was thinking I knew what my audience wanted.

Instead, I had to *discover* who my ideal audience was.

You can do all those popular "customer avatar" exercises, and tell yourself that your ideal client is a 43 year old mother of four, loves to knit and cries every time she sees a *Hallmark* movie on TV, but in reality, you're just guessing until the *marketplace* responds to your content and offerings.

Absolutely, you should have a target or niche audience in mind when you *start* creating and sharing your content (and selling your products and services) online. And yes, you should factor in things like age, gender, industry type, job title or role and so on.

But the bigger factor (in my experience, at least) is to *adjust* that customer avatar based on *who actually purchases your products and services.* Especially if you are launching a new product or service, it's critical, once you make a few sales, to really analyze who your buyers are.

Do this by asking your new customers questions. How did they find you? What *specifically* was appealing about your content or approach that convinced them you were the answer? What are their biggest hopes, dreams or difficulties - personally or professionally - right now?

Your customers will be happy to tell you what ails them and what they need help with. You just need to ask!

Creating effective content comes down to solving problems. And once you get some consensus from your buyers and customers on what those core challenges are, then you have the strategic direction you need for your future content marketing efforts.

To summarize: In the beginning, make your best *guess* based on what you think is your ideal audience, and then *adjust* based on who actually buys your products and services.

The Curse of Generality

Now, you might be thinking, "Well, my product or service is for everybody!"

You might spend time telling yourself all the ways people of all ages and backgrounds can benefit from your products and services, and, in a perfect world, that's likely true.

Even more, you might be able to create content that engages multiple audiences and gets them hooked (remember the fishing analogy from earlier?) into your world online.

However, will these people actually *buy* your products and services?

(Remember, you can't deposit positive blog comments, shares or "likes" on social media into your bank account.)

What I Discovered Selling Online Courses

For example, when I first set out to sell online training courses ranging in price from $997 USD to $2997 USD, I began by creating content that would appeal to anyone from 25 to 75 years of age in any type of corporate setting.

What I quickly discovered was that if someone worked inside a large company (or even a small one), it took a lot of phone calls and hand-holding to help the person get approval from his or her boss to purchase my online course.

One woman inside a huge insurance company spent nine months(!) working internally to get approval to purchase my LinkedIn Riches online course.

I quickly realized that my *best* customers, the ones who had the least amount of friction when it came to consuming my free content (books, blogs, webinars, etc.) and then purchasing my paid offerings, were self-employed Business Coaches and Consultants over 40 years of age.

That specific audience (Coaches and Consultants) didn't have the red tape that corporate employees did - if they were on my webinar, liked what they saw and wanted to take advantage of a time-sensitive offer, they did.

Because they were self-employed and self-starters, these Business Coaches and Consultants didn't have any qualms about investing in their own education if they believed it would bring their business real ROI.

Also, because they put their own money on the line, these individuals were the most motivated to complete my online courses and take action. As a result, they became star students, getting measurable results and turning into case studies I could use to market my online courses to other Business Coaches and Consultants.

On the flip side, while my content marketing generated tons of interest and engagement with corporate employees, inevitably I got sucked into a black hole of conference calls, back-and-forth emails and more selling to try and convince someone's boss my online course was a good investment of the company's time and money.

I had many conversations, for example, with corporate sales professionals who told me something along these lines: "So, I love your LinkedIn training, I totally see how it would work awesome for our company, but I have to convince my boss that it makes sense. He doesn't 'get' LinkedIn, and I'm not sure how to explain it to him. Can you spend time on the phone helping me convince him we should do this?"

I was putting in all this extra work on sales calls that sometimes panned out, and often didn't, because the person I'd convinced with my *content* (the sales professional) wasn't the one who had the final buying authority for my products and services.

Instead, I found myself thrust into what amounted to cold calls with skeptical, busy and distracted bosses looking to save budget dollars and find a reason not to trust me or my programs.

So, once I understood who my actual *buyers* were, I began creating content to meet *their* specific needs.

I stopped worrying about the 25 to 35 year old corporate sales or marketing employee and instead focused on the 40 to 75 year old Business Coach or solo Consultant.

I also realized that, given the age range of my buyers, I could incorporate 1980's and 1990's-themed pop culture references and humor into my content.

I knew an audience in that age range would "get" all my 1980's jokes about tube socks and running to the video arcade with a pocket full of quarters, or the early 1990's fashion faux paux committed by my sisters and I with our rolled jeans, spiked bangs and leather bomber jackets.

When you know who your audience is, what era they grew up in and what they want personally and professionally, creating content becomes much easier and more effective as a result.

Now, maybe you already know who your buyers (and therefore, your target audiences) are.

If so, make sure you really dig deeply into what makes them tick before you go out and create content aimed at them. Try your best to get into their heads (what drives them) and their hearts (what motivates them or makes them emotional).

For example, if you know your target audience is young, stay-at-home mothers, content that's focused on parenting and improving the lives of your children is going to capture their time and attention quite well. Especially if you can "humanize" it with stories of real moms with real kids and real challenges similar to those your target audience faces.

And then, placing your product or service as a solution to that common problem is where the content marketing magic happens.

Ask. Create. Repeat.

Sure, it can be a lot of work, but I've found that surveying my buyers and asking them questions not only strengthens and deepens our relationship, but it also gives me countless ideas, angles and directions for creating content that will convert.

Remember, you have to create content that is both *aspirational* (appealing to the goals, dreams and emotions of your audience) and *practical* (actual tips that help them accomplish a task or meet a need).

The only way you know for sure what your ideal audience wants is to ask them!

The One Question Survey

One of my favorite methods for this is called The One Question Survey.

In fact, I used it to create the title and content of the very book you hold in your hands right now!

The One Question Survey consists of just nine words, but it has permanently changed the way I create, sell and market my products online.

In fact, this one question dictates how I build intricate online courses, craft marketing and email copy and much more.

Before I reveal what it is, I must re-emphasize why it is so important to utilize this approach in your business.

Your Customers Care About ... Themselves!

One of the biggest mistakes you can make in creating and/or marketing a product or service online (or anywhere else) is not first *asking* your ideal customer what he or she wants.

"People are not interested in you. They are not interested in me," wrote Dale Carnegie in his 1936 Bestseller *How To Win Friends and Influence People*. "They are interested in themselves – morning, noon and after dinner."

"The point is this," adds David J. Schwartz in another bestselling business book, *The Magic of Thinking Big*. "To get others to do what you want them to do, you must see things through their eyes."

A perfect (and real life) example of this situation happened for me in creating this very book.

As I began to plan out this book (and an online course designed to take what you read here even further), I thought I knew *exactly* where my audience was with this topic of Content Marketing.

Boy, was I wrong!

Before I explain what happened, let's dive into what this customer survey strategy is and how to utilize it.

Again, it's called "The 1 Question Survey," and I first discovered it via an online course creator named David Siteman Garland.

When you deploy this simple survey strategy, not only do you learn *what* your ideal audience actually wants you to create and/or sell to them, you also discover *how* they want you to communicate to them about it (meaning the words and phrases to use.)

Last (and most important!), you are able to close the gap between what you *think* your ideal customer knows and wants versus what he or she *actually says*.

In my case, with my this new book and online course on Content Marketing, I just assumed my current customers already knew what the topic was all about, and that they were more interested in the "how to" type questions about utilizing it.

I was in for a giant surprise, as I'll share in a bit.

The 1 Question Survey

First, here's the template you can utilize for the 1 Question Survey:

"What do you want to know more about [BLANK]?"

You just replace "BLANK" with the topic you want the audience to tell you about.

Another variation I like to use is swapping in the word "most" for "more," so it reads like this:

"What do you want to know most about [BLANK]?"

In my case, I wrote this:

"What do you want to know most about Content Marketing?"

Next, I set up a simple (and free) survey via Google Forms, and (this is important!) I did not ask for anyone's name, email or contact information.

Instead, it was just that one simple question – fast and easy, plus anonymity to encourage honesty.

Here's what it looked like on Google Forms:

Next, I sent the following email to my customers, linking to the survey:

(Subject Line): quick question

(Email Body): So I have one quick, burning question I'd love to get your answer to.

It should only take you a few seconds, and it's something you'll definitely want to answer.

Answer my 1 quick question here.

Thanks in advance – I'm excited to read your answers!

— John Nemo

The Response That Shocked Me

Here's where I was in for a big surprise.

Again, I'd just had this assumption that everyone in my customer base already "got" or "knew" what Content Marketing was all about.

Instead, several of my customers wrote variations of this answer:

"I don't know what that term means."

"What exactly is Content Marketing?"

"How do you define it?"

Wow!

So that issue became something I could address right away in my content and sales copy:

"What is Content Marketing? (And Why Should You Care?)"

Had I not run the 1 Question Survey prior to starting this book and online course (and all the marketing efforts behind it), I would have had a major disconnect with my existing customers and not realized why.

After all, nobody wants to a buy a course on a topic they don't fully "get," right?

This is why I love doing the 1 Question Survey before I create a new product, put together sales copy for a specific type of product or anything else.

How To Use The 1 Question Survey

You can utilize this strategy anywhere and anytime … in a LinkedIn message, an email blast to existing clients or prospects, as a social media post on Facebook asking for feedback, and so on.

I suggest using a tool like Google Forms and directing everyone there to share his or her answer, because then you get an organized list of responses you can download and examine.

Study (And Apply) The Results!

Even more important than the survey itself is actually studying and applying the results to your copywriting and marketing efforts.

Once I get enough responses to feel like I have a consensus on some topics, I go into my project management software (Basecamp) and create a list of the top themes I see, along with great "quotes" people utilized in their specific answers.

Here's an example from my survey results of top "themes" I saw in this survey:

CUSTOMER Phrases / Wants

THEMES
- What is Content Marketing?
- How To Get Your Target Audience to Consume Your Content
- How to use it to generate leads
- Step-by-Step approach / how to systemize
- How to make it simple
- One and done: How to create evergreen content
- Idea Factory: How to think of or come up with content ideas
- Content Marketing Calendar // Planning
- How to stick with it
- How to continue to make the content interesting and relevant to the audience / how to know what your audience wants!
- Content Curation? how to source & automate content sharing
- Optimal Length of article?
- Paid vs. free content

And here are some "quotes" I highlighted from the answers:

KEY QUOTES

- Would like a minimalistic method that works. The "minimum effective dose" so to speak, because as you know preparing quality content takes time. So what is the leanest approach to doing content marketing that works.
- How to continue to make the content interesting and relevant to the audience
- How to keep going when you're sick of writing about the same topic and are running out of ideas for new angles to talk about it.
- How to think of content to write about
- What really is Content Marketing? :-) The terminology is bandied about in so many different ways it can leave one confused about its objective and how it is used.
- The best way to plan it -- a content marketing calendar? How do you create one? How do you stick to it? How do you find/create content in time to meet the deadlines you'd planned in your content marketing calendar?
- What is the secret to curation?
- How do I know what content my audience values?
- I now lots. What I struggle with is implementation. I wonder, what about a step-by-step hand-holding course ("Today, we do this...)
- The balance between free content and paid content - what works for you.
- How to make it irresistible!

Now, when I went out to create landing pages, email copy and bullet points for content associated with this topic, I had *specific words and phrases* straight from the mouths of my customers to utilize.

This is important: When you create content and sales copy to promote your products and services, you want to *use the same language* your customers do. (Remember the headline example with Chiropractors and "patients" instead of "customers"?)

Simple and Effective

It's easy to skip right over the step of actually *asking* your ideal clients and customers what they want or how they want to be marketed to, especially if you think you know it all.

Don't make this mistake!

As Schwartz points out in *The Magic of Thinking Big,* you need to "trade minds" with your audience.

"When you trade minds, the secret of how to influence other people effectively shows up," he writes. "Keep this question in mind: 'What would I think of this if I exchanged places with the other person?' It paves the way to more successful action."

Having written his bestselling book back in 1959, Schwartz had no idea of the advantages we have in today's technological wonderland.

Make sure you take advantage and utilize the 1 Question Survey approach accordingly.

Pivot Your "Pitch" into Creative Content

As I explained earlier with the example of selling your video marketing services to chiropractors, the key in creating effective content is eschewing traditional sales pitches and instead positioning your product or service as a solution to a problem.

Once you understand the biggest pain points and problems your customers have, you can place your product or service as a fast, easy and effective solution to those challenges.

Even better is doing it with content that tells a powerful story - one complete with real characters, real challenges and (of course) a happy ending.

As I mentioned earlier, telling great stories is what sells your products and services. Science has shown that our brains encode a great story in a way where we can remember the lessons, characters and outcome for a long, long time.

Facts can fall in and out of our consciousness like waves hitting an ocean shore, sliding in and then retreating back into the sea of information they came from.

Stories, however, are sticky. Even better, they trigger emotions, and making someone *emotional* is critical to building a bond that goes beyond a simple exchange of information.

Putting it into Practice

Here's an example of how I utilized this approach in my own content marketing efforts.

From customer surveys, I know one of the biggest challenges one of my target audiences (Business Coaches) often face is finding (and pre-qualifying) new clients in an effective fashion.

I also know that LinkedIn is the best platform on the planet for Business Coaches to find, engage and pre-qualify potential clients without having to spend countless hours playing professional footsie via networking events, coffee meetings or other time-consuming efforts.

From Case Study to Inspiring Story

As a result, I decided to take one of my star LinkedIn Riches students, a Business Coach named Bill Prater, and tell his story via a blog post.

Since I wanted to market this piece of content specifically to Business Coaches, I needed an actual Business Coach (i.e., Bill) to be the main character and "hero" of my story.

So, in what amounts to a case study of how Bill used my LinkedIn Riches online course to win himself a bunch of new business, I told his story in the form of a blog post that I knew would resonate with that specific target audience of Business Coaches.

And, in a topic I'll touch on more in-depth later on, I decided to record and repurpose Bill's story in multiple formats (video, audio and text) to maximize the value of my content.

I started by recording a Skype conversation with Bill sharing his story, and then turned snippets of it into a testimonial video for my sales webinar, along with releasing a longer version of the entire conversation as an episode of my audio podcast.

Finally, I had the audio from our Skype call transcribed, and then used the written record of our conversation to create a blog post.

Here's how the blog looked:

How a Business Coach Landed a $90k Client Using LinkedIn

He called it "borderline worthless."

He was frustrated, fed up and flummoxed.

In short, Bill Prater, a Business Coach based in Seattle, Washington, was struggling to get people he found online to become paid coaching clients.

For someone who had already built a successful coaching and consulting business pre-Internet, Prater, like many, was struggling to translate those lead generation practices into the digital marketplace.

"I felt the whole social media marketing thing was so inauthentic," he told me in a recent Nemo Radio Podcast episode.

"But using this (specific type of) approach on LinkedIn, it enabled me to use the Internet in an authentic way that I'd been using for 15 years, but had always believed I had to be face-to-face with somebody."

Within 60 days of applying "that approach" on LinkedIn, Prater had landed a new client worth $90,000, along with several other new clients for his lower-tiered coaching programs.

In addition, he so filled his prospect pipeline that he now has a waiting list of potential clients wanting to talk with him.

The way he did it is what we'll spend the rest of this post on.

LinkedIn + Authenticity = New Business

Because Prater is providing a B2B service, there is no better place online to find new prospects than LinkedIn.

With 550 million members in 200 countries, and with 2 new members joining every second, using LinkedIn to generate leads is a no-brainer for those in the B2B space.

LinkedIn fancies itself as a "one stop shop" for professionals worldwide, with the platform providing industry-specific news and views, online training programs, a freelance project and vendor database, professional groups, job openings and more.

Knowing that the people he connected with on LinkedIn were already there in "work" mode, Prater realized his prospecting time was better spent there than on Facebook or other "non-work" social media platforms.

Even better, because LinkedIn indexes every piece of professional data (from your entire profile page to status updates and blog posts) published on the site, it has one of the world's most powerful (and valuable) Search Engines built right into the platform.

For example, you can type in the job title or role of the person you want to connect with inside LinkedIn's search box, hit enter and instantly get a result of thousands (if not millions) of people who do that type of work.

Even better, you can use LinkedIn's advanced search filters to narrow your list of results based on someone's physical location, company name, industry type or even where he or she went to school.

Selling on LinkedIn = Personalized, 1-on-1 Marketing

The result is the ability to conduct what I call 1-on-1, personalized marketing.

It's the core foundation of my LinkedIn training courses and the secret to using LinkedIn to generate qualified, engaged and "ready to buy" sales leads.

Here's how it works: Because you can *instantly* see from a person's LinkedIn profile where he or she lives, works, went to school, etc., you can *immediately* engage him or her in a personal, authentic and friendly fashion.

"Historically, I'd been relying on face-to-face interactions," Prater says. "Because my business is extremely based on trust. And so I found that I can build that relationship if I have a one-on-one relationship with somebody. Meet them for coffee, or lunch, etc."

With LinkedIn, Prater could now take that 1-on-1, personalized approach and instantly connect in a personal fashion thanks to LinkedIn providing all that information up front.

He was able to do it without leaving his laptop, driving all over town for coffee meetings or playing what I call "professional footsie" with potential clients.

"Using this approach, I've been able to successfully convert what I'll call 'cold' prospects, people who I've never met and found on LinkedIn," he says.

LinkedIn Messaging = Know, Like & Trust

Following the advice I share in regards to LinkedIn training for business, Prater nurtures prospects along with a series of back-and-forth, 1-on-1 LinkedIn messages.

He spends around 30-40 minutes per day on LinkedIn finding, connecting and messaging his ideal clients on the platform.

Again, because of your ability to cut through the clutter and go directly to the *exact* people you want to reach, and then engage in a 1-on-1, personalized fashion, your time is maximized on LinkedIn in a way you cannot replicate offline.

Here's an example: Once you connect with someone on LinkedIn, the platform allows you to message each other back and forth in real-time, similar to texting. You can even see when someone else is typing or has read your messages on LinkedIn.

Using this tool, Prater and his prospects get to know, like and trust one another quickly, and in a non-threatening, non-salesy, non-spammy fashion.

Prater uses pre-written invite and messaging scripts to ask new connections about their business, their biggest challenges and needs, and then looks for ways he can add value based on his business coaching knowledge and expertise.

Since he's pre-qualified his prospects using LinkedIn Search, Prater already knows if someone is likely going to be in a position to benefit from his training and coaching services.

Based on how all these "real-time" conversations go over on LinkedIn, Prater can then move a person *off* LinkedIn and onto the telephone.

He offers a free "discovery call" to dive deeper, and because these once "cold" prospects are now warmed up via LinkedIn, it makes the call a natural extension of the messaging experience.

"It's been an eye-opening experience," Prater says. "My dance card of clients, so to speak, is now full. And it's been the ability to use the Internet in a way that is genuine, authentic and legitimately helpful to the people I'm speaking with."

Want To Replicate Bill's Approach on LinkedIn?

Then you need to register for one of my free online training sessions!

Click below to get started:

Free Training: How To Generate Nonstop Sales Leads, Clients and Revenue with LinkedIn ... FAST!

(Author's Note: The hyperlinked text above goes to this link: https://linkedinriches.com/webinar-coaching/)

Content Marketing Demystified

In short, creating the type of content your audience will go bananas for comes down to simply *asking* them, then creating content that meets their needs and solves their problems in a way that is *also* entertaining and memorable.

Telling great stories is a key part of this process, and one we'll dive into more deeply in the chapters to come.

For now, if you want to get yourself a "quick win" from this chapter, go out and deploy the "1 Question Survey" with some of your clients or customers online.

I'm betting some of their insights and answers will not only surprise you, but spur some great ideas inside your mind of new content you can create as a result!

Chapter 4:
Gone Fishin' - How to Set Up a Sales Funnel Using Content

I still can feel my father's enormous, obnoxious and thoroughly 1970's plastic stereo headphones slipped over my 3 year old ears, mesmerized as the sounds of *The Beatles* slid into my mind and mesmerized me.

I remember opening the double doors of my father's large, wooden stereo cabinet and pulling out countless records. I'd place one on the player, watching the needle gently touch down onto the grooved record, and feeling my ears fill with incredible sounds.

Once I'd heard one song, I had to listen to another. And another. Soon, I'd have gone through an entire album in one sitting, relaxing in my father's lime green recliner with those obscene headphones covering my tiny head like some sort of space alien.

Here, I even have proof:

(If that image doesn't scream late 1970's, I don't know what does!)

If you're a music fan, think about when you discover a new song from a band you've never heard of before. What's the first thing you do?

If you're like me, you immediately want to consume *more* of their content (i.e., songs). And, if you like those songs, you end up buying an entire album. Maybe even a concert ticket.

And, once you see the band live and get that whole experience, now you're completely hooked. You join their fan club, pay for early access to their new music, buy their merchandise, tell all your friends how great they are, and so on.

And all of it started from one piece of content.

This chapter is about how to build a sales funnel with content, and I love that music analogy as a way to introduce the topic.

Because, in essence, this is how a content marketing funnel works. A person sees one piece of your content somewhere, and, if he or she likes it, she typically wants to consume more. And, eventually, depending on how your funnel is structured, that journey results in a paid exchange.

Funnels of Fun

Depending on your product or service and price points, you can create very simple (and short) sales funnels or very long and involved ones.

It all goes back to this: *How much trust do you have to earn with someone in order to justify the asking price for your service or product?*

There's a big difference between selling a $14.95 USD book and a $1,497.00 USD online course.

The higher your price tag, the more complex and value-driven your sales funnel needs to be.

Structuring Your Sales Funnel

Depending on how you like to create your content, and how your ideal audience likes to consume it, there are several directions you can go with building out your funnel.

Regardless, I cannot emphasize enough how important it is for you to "own" and "control" your sales funnel and leads. The best way to do this is by getting people to opt-in to an email list that you build and have ownership of.

As tempting as it is to house your audience on one of the popular social media platforms that millions of people use each day, it's also quite dangerous.

For example, if you *only* build a huge following of subscribers on YouTube and *only* utilize YouTube's platform to deliver your content to and communicate with your audience, what happens if YouTube changes the rules on you?

What if YouTube one day says, "Hey, now we're going to make you pay to reach your subscribers" or something else?

This happened with Facebook fan pages a few years ago, and caused great consternation and online bellyaching as a result.

But, here's the deal: Facebook owns that digital sandbox and all of its toys. You don't. So, if they want to change the rules overnight, they can, and you're powerless to stop them.

The same is true of any social network, and that's why my main goal is to always get people I meet on social networks *off that network and onto my email list instead.*

I literally built my entire business using LinkedIn, but my main focus when I connect with someone on the world's largest platform for professionals is always to get them *off of LinkedIn* and over to my email list via a free piece of content like an eBook, webinar or something similar.

What a Simple Content Marketing Funnel Looks Like

With that said, let's move into what an actual sales funnel can look like and how content plays a key part.

Going back to our fishing analogy from earlier in the book, you have to create some initial content that will serve as "bait" for all those prospects swimming around the digital sea.

If you've done your homework (defining your target audience, deploying the 1 Question Survey, etc.), then you should have a good idea of what topics are going to catch the time, interest and attention of your audience.

Next, you'll want to structure your content in a way where it can give people a "quick win" and is simple to accomplish. One of the most popular (and effective) pieces of content I ever created was my "Ultimate LinkedIn Profile Template," which is copy-and-paste simple and easy to execute.

People see an immediate result and get some instant gratification by improving their LinkedIn profile without much pain or effort, and that opens them up to wanting to hear more from me.

When *starting* your sales funnel, you want to find a piece of "quick win" content (like my LinkedIn Profile Template) that will give your audience a tangible result with minimal effort.

Let me repeat this, because it is critical: *Your initial piece of content should promise (and deliver) your audience a tangible (and desirable) result with minimal effort on their part.*

People Want Simple, Fast and Easy

I learned this lesson the hard way when offering up two similar pieces of content to the same audience.

One piece of content was a series in-depth training videos that shared some of my best tips and tactics for creating a killer LinkedIn profile.

The *positioning* of that content made it clear on the landing page that these training videos went deep, and that you'd learn a lot in this *series* of online videos.

The other piece of content was a short eBook ("The Ultimate LinkedIn Profile Template") that was positioned as fast, easy and simple:

"Get the EXACT words, phrases and formatting hacks … copy-and-paste simple … takes just a few minutes to apply!"

Both pieces of content promised the same result (a killer LinkedIn profile), but the eBook *sounded* much easier and simple to execute, and as a result it generated way more email opt-ins.

Never forget that people love the path of least resistance. When given the choice of doing something easy or hard and getting a similar outcome, they will choose the easier path!

Perception = Reality

Once you figure out what that initial piece of content is going to be, you need to create it, of course, and (more importantly) *position* and *present* it as something of real value.

For example, I first published "The Ultimate LinkedIn Profile Template" eBook as a simple blog post on my website.

There was no fancy formatting, no fancy graphics and no opt-in required to access the material.

While the content was great, the *positioning* and *presentation* was not.

As a result, that particular piece of content (a free blog post) did very little to grow my business or fill up my sales funnel with email subscribers.

However, when I turned that same blog post into a formatted eBook, complete with some fancy formatting and graphics, the same content was now being *presented* as something of much higher value.

In addition, I changed the *positioning* of the content as well, putting the "Ultimate Template" eBook behind an email opt-in requirement instead of just giving away the content for free to anyone and everyone.

Making it a requirement to opt-in to access the eBook immediately *positioned* the content as higher-value, or at least gave the *perception* that the content was higher-value.

Making an Exchange

This is key, because asking someone for his or her email address is almost like asking for money - there is now an *exchange* taking place. Your reader or viewer is putting some skin (giving you his or her email address) into the game, and he or she is now more invested and interested to see if your content lives up to the *perceived value* he or she is assigning it.

Think about it - if someone gives you something for free, with no effort or "payment" on your part, you may or may not pay close attention and utilize it.

After all, it was free, so who cares if you get too busy or distracted to really dig deep into that particular piece of content?

And, because it was free, you might think, *was the content really that valuable?*

Whereas, if you had to enter your email to access the content, you're far more likely to give it a closer look, because in your mind, the *perceived* value is higher, along with the fact that you had to put in some effort or "payment" (giving away your email address) to access it.

Please note, I'm *not* saying you should make every piece of content you create require a reader or viewer to opt-in to access it.

However, when building out a simple sales funnel, you *do* need to create, present and position your content as *valuable* enough to require an email opt-in to access it.

Getting someone to opt-in and join your email list is key, because that gives you permission to begin a *relationship* with the other person, sending them additional content now that you have their *permission* to do so.

Going back to the amount of trust required to sell your product or service, you can't simply give away a free eBook and then expect someone to immediately purchase your $1,500 USD online course or hire you as a Business Coach.

Instead, you must *nurture* someone along inside your sales funnel, using your *content* to engage, entertain and inspire the person to believe that not only can you help them, but that they will *enjoy* working with you to achieve their goals.

You've Got Mail - What Effective Email Marketing Looks Like

Once someone opts in to receive more of your content, we move into the magical realm of email marketing.

The logistics of email marketing are simple enough: You use an email service provider to collect the emails of people who opt-in to access your content, and then you set up automated sequences of follow-up messages that nurture the person along with more emails, eventually inviting them to purchase one of your products or services.

For example, once a person opts-in to access "The Ultimate LinkedIn Profile Template," they immediately get an email that delivers the PDF along with a welcome note introducing them to me.

Next, they get put onto an automated sequence of follow up email messages, each one building off of that initial eBook's content to take them further into my sales funnel, going beyond how to create a killer LinkedIn profile and moving into how to find, engage and sell to their ideal clients on the platform.

Finally, at various points during the email autoresponder series, they get invited to an automated webinar where I dive deeper into LinkedIn lead generation tips and present a special, time-sensitive offer to join my LinkedIn Riches Online Course near the end of the webinar.

The whole process involves about a dozen different pre-written emails that I send out over a 30 day period, mixing in tips, sharing my story and inviting engagement, and ultimately inviting them to purchase my online course after viewing the automated webinar.

(Note: To get direct access to my highest-converting emails and to see how I set up a sequence, go to https://ContentMarketingMachine.com/Bonus)

Keep in mind, I'm selling a high-ticket ($1,500 USD to $2,000 USD) online course, so I have to do a lot of work over those 30 days to build up the "know, like and trust" elements necessary to any business transaction.

Depending on what your ultimate "ask" is, you don't necessarily need a huge email sequence with dozens of emails spread out over several weeks.

For example, if you're a Business Coach, maybe your goal is to get someone on the phone for a free 15 minute discovery call. In that case, perhaps offering one free (and really well done!) piece of content is enough to entice the person to book a free call with you to talk more about your approach and see if it makes sense for his or her business.

In that instance, you wouldn't even need to build an email funnel. Instead, you could just finish your blog post with a Call To Action (CTA) that includes your website, phone number or a link to your online calendar to book a phone call.

For a Business Coach or Consultant who does his or her best work to win new business on the phone, using a value-packed blog that delivers some quick wins *and* demonstrates your expertise and insight is also a great way to "pre-qualify" potential clients.

After all, someone has to *first* read through your blog post and consume your content before getting to the bottom, where your CTA has a link to your online calendar and/or your direct contact info.

Analyze This

Experiment with an approach like this one and see what the results are. Do the folks booking discovery calls end up being great prospects, or are most just unqualified tire kickers?

One key approach with Content Marketing is to always *analyze and adjust.* You need to take a specific approach, deploy a strategy and study the results.

Keeping in mind the earlier lessons of this book, including this one: The more your free content drills directly into the deep desires or problems of a specific, target audience you want to serve, the more likely the people consuming that content and booking follow-up phone calls with you are going to become customers.

Either way, the key in building out a simple sales funnel with content is making sure your *initial* offering hits that sweet spot of promising a desirable result with minimal effort.

If you can do that, you'll have no problem getting people to share their emails or book discovery calls as a result.

If your ask is "larger" than a quick phone call and involves higher-end, more expensive services or pricing, then you need to create a more complex and content-rich sales funnel.

You still *start* the same, with your first piece of content delivering a quick win that requires minimal effort on the audience's part. But after that, you need to get more nuanced and strategic with the follow up content you send someone who has opted in to receive your emails and content.

Practice Professional Courtship

One massive mistake far too many people make with content marketing is trying to marry someone on the first date.

Again, if you're looking to sell a high-end product or service, you can't simply give someone a free eBook or single training video and then pitch them on forking over thousands of dollars for your online course or consulting services.

Instead, you've got to take each person on a journey, moving beyond that first "quick win" piece of content to deliver more depth, value and insight into why working with you or utilizing your services is a no-brainer.

With email marketing and content delivery, you want to move people along a continuum, bringing them on a journey from small, quick and easy wins into heavier (and far more valuable) content that gets them to their ideal results.

How it Works

For example, when I want to ultimately sell someone my LinkedIn Riches Online Course, I first get the person onto my email list by offering up a lead magnet like "The Ultimate LinkedIn Profile Template."

Knowing my ideal audience by now, and *where* they are at online, I've come to realize most people need to *start* the journey by improving their existing LinkedIn profile.

The "Ultimate Profile" eBook helps them do that, and (this is important!) that quick win helps a person feel a sense of accomplishment and momentum as the journey begins.

When you start by improving your LinkedIn profile, I explain in my emails that follow the eBook, it's like cleaning up and remodeling your house online. And, once your virtual house is clean, shiny and looking spectacular, it's time to throw a party and invite people over to see the finished product!

So, in my ensuing emails, I help the reader *continue the momentum* they began with by moving into how to find, engage and talk to their ideal prospects on LinkedIn.

Bolstered by the confidence and excitement of having something of value (a client-attracting LinkedIn profile) to point prospects to on the platform, readers are eager for the next steps in the process.

Share Your Story

At this point, I need to mention, it's *not* just enough to share great strategies and tips with your emails and follow-up content. You also need to weave *your* personal story and journey into your content and tips.

Your new email subscribers need to feel like they can relate to you, and sharing the journey you took to get to where you are today helps make you relatable, trustworthy and likable.

This is often called "The Hero's Journey," and it needs to be a critical part of your content inside a more complex sales funnel.

"Start with your audiences and their needs, then introduce yourself as a *catalyst* for helping them meet those needs, and a story instantly begins to unfold," writes Jonah Sachs in his book *Winning The Story Wars*. "[Create] conflict between your audience's desires and their current state. And a plot or journey that you invite them to join you on to reach those desires."

The idea here is to show (via sharing your story) the journey you went on with this particular topic (in my case, using LinkedIn to generate sales leads and win new business), and *how your audience can do the exact same thing*.

"Marketers must help audiences to see themselves as the emerging heroes of the story," Sachs writes. "Everything you need is already inside, these stories say; we can help you on your journey to actualize your potential. The core strategy of empowerment marketing is not about magical fulfillment. It's about values and inspiration."

Sharing your story of adversity and the obstacles you overcame to achieve this new reality helps your audience believe that *they can do it, too*.

Here's an example of one of the first emails I send new subscribers around LinkedIn:

Subject Line: my big (LinkedIn) secret

Email Text:

Back in 2012, I was terrified.

I was also excited.

I'd just quit my safe, 6 figure day job to start my own business from scratch.

I had 1 client, enough money for 30 days and a stay-at-home wife and 3 young boys to support.

(That would be the "terrified" part.)

I also had a plan.

(That would be the "excited" part.)

The Result --

Within 90 days of quitting my day job, I'd generated $135,000 in revenue from new clients I found on LinkedIn.

In the emails to come, I'm going to show you EXACTLY how I did it.

And, more important, how YOU can do the same thing.

(It's far easier than you think.)

For now, I want to know something more important than sales or income.

I want to know your WHY.

Why do you do what you do? What gets you out of bed in the morning? What motivates you?

When I quit my day job back in 2012, this was my "why":

To spend more time with my wife and our 3 young sons.

Reply right now and answer this question for me ...

What's your "why?"

I can't wait to hear from you!

- John Nemo, LinkedIn Riches

Note how in this first email I'm sharing my "Hero's Journey" - the huge risk I took, the obstacles I had to overcome and the great result I achieved by using LinkedIn to grow my business.

Note also how I'm making it *personal* for my reader: *"What's your 'Why?'"*

I want to hook into your emotional center right away, to get you thinking about the desired *result* that you could achieve if you were able to grow your business quickly using a tool like LinkedIn.

When you start envisioning more family time, or having more freedom to travel the world and take vacations, or whatever else it might be, *now* you're more invested in and excited about the process.

Finally, notice how I don't go overboard in this first email with tons of information, strategy and insights.

Rather, I make it clear I believe in my reader ("You can do the EXACT same thing!") and promise to reveal *how* to accomplish the goal in future emails.

This initial message works well because (A) It makes people emotional about using LinkedIn to achieve an important goal (their "Why"), (B) Generates engagement by inviting them to share their "Why" with me and (C) Makes me approachable, relatable and likable because I'm admitting I didn't start out as some LinkedIn guru who had it all figured out.

Finally, I'm making sure I *humanize* myself by sharing a photo of me hugging my three young boys - putting a visual exclamation point on the "Why" that drove me to utilize LinkedIn this way.

(Note: To get access to all my favorite email templates and the specific emails I send as part of the LinkedIn Riches sequence, go to https://ContentMarketingMachine.com/Bonus)

Building Out Your Email Funnel

Now that the stage has been set, the next emails inside my autoresponder sequence start to reveal strategies, tips and tactics my reader can use to generate some momentum and "quick wins" when it comes to using LinkedIn to generate leads and add new customers.

However, I always mix in personal stories and photos whenever possible to illustrate those strategies and methods, because it continues to make me relatable, likeable and trustworthy in the eyes of my audience.

"If you can form a relationship with your customers based on shared values, that is the strongest possible bond you can form," Sachs writes in *Winning The Story Wars*. "But finding shared values means you have to *have* some values, they can't just be milquetoast, namby-pamby middle-of-the-road [junk]. You need to stand for something, so customers who believe the same thing can glom onto your brand."

What Do YOU Stand For?

I want to stay here for a moment longer, because injecting your personality and passion into your emails and other content is just as important as the actual strategies, tips and valuable information you share.

Taking a strong stand and planting your flag in the ground for a certain set of values or aspirations is critical to helping you and your personal brand stand out in a crowded marketplace.

It also helps you attract an ideal audience - one who agrees with your core values and wants the same thing you do!

Your Values = Your Audience's Values

For example, here's the shared values I want to build my ideal audience around:

Value 1: No Boss. No Office. Call Your Own Shots.

Value 2: Given today's tools and technology, there's ZERO reason you can't turn your passion into a paying business.

Value 3: *Expect* to Fail, Learn and Adjust. Don't Quit. Don't Make Excuses. Do the Work.

Value 4: Transfer your offline expertise into an online marketplace. (Online courses, etc.)

Listen Up

Just like I first fell in love with music as a three year old wearing my dad's oversized stereo headphones, people will fall in love with *your* brand and business based on the content you create and share.

Like songs on an album, the content you create for your sales funnel should be stitched together so that those individual items combine to tell a larger story and lead people to a specific outcome.

A series of automated emails is the easiest way to achieve this, and structuring those messages to deliver the right mixture of tips and tactics while sharing your personal "Hero's Journey" is critical to ensuring the sequence is effective.

Finally, it's all about understanding how much (and what type) of content is needed to "earn" the trust of someone based on what you're ultimate "ask" will be. The bigger the price tag for your product or service, the more powerful and value-packed your content sequence needs to be.

Rock on!

Chapter 5:
Create vs. Curate - Which One Should You Do?

It's a question asked often, and one where the answer will vary quite a bit depending on whom you ask: *Is it better to create content or to curate it?*

To me, there is no debate - not if you want to be viewed as the authority and expert in your respective arena.

Creating content is where it's at.

Simply put, *nothing* can replicate the expertise, authority and personality that shines through when you create great (and original) content.

Not creating your own content is like putting out a Podcast without a voice, or writing a book without words.

Like it or not, in today's online marketplace, *you need to create your own original, unique and valuable content to be successful.*

In fact, content is the core driver of all your sales, marketing, branding and revenue efforts.

Excuse Me?

Also, I don't buy the "I'm not a writer, I'm not a professional speaker, so I don't know how to create content" excuse I hear all too often.

My answer is always the same: *Can you communicate? Can you speak?*

Then you can create content. I'll go into more detail later on, but there are countless ways to create great content *without* having to be a bestselling author, professional speaker or on-camera movie star.

When Curating Content Makes Sense

Now, that's not to say there's zero value in curating content and delivering it to a target audience.

For instance, I subscribe to a weekly email newsletter from a PR professional who curates the biggest PR and Marketing stories from around the industry and shares them every Friday via email.

It's a fun, fast and easy way for me to peruse the top trends people are talking about.

At the same time, I don't really *know, like or trust* the person curating the content beyond the few opening lines he shares in his email or in his comments about some of the stories he links to.

Worst of all, he's pointing me *away* from himself and to someone else's content and platform.

Now, if this person took an additional step and started sending me more of his *original* content to supplement his curation efforts, then things would get good.

Because this person has "earned" a spot in my inbox and stays "top of mind" with me each Friday via that email of curated stories, he has a golden opportunity to move the relationship further by having me focus on *his* original content.

At the end of the day, curating content can be a great way to stay in front of people and provide some value. Just realize that people can use Google to do the same thing.

On the flipside, *nobody* can replicate or replace your original, unique content and voice online. And that, dear reader, is where all the magic happens.

Before I end this brief chapter, if you're one of those "But I'm not good at creating content" believers, take a deep breath and relax.

You actually *are* capable of creating great content … maybe you just don't know *how* to do it yet. And I'll show you exactly how to make that happen it in the chapters to come.

The *key* is understanding how to get all the expertise, knowledge and insights you possess in that beautiful brain of yours out into a form of content that entertains, engages and inspires your ideal audience.

And, as we explore moving forward, you'll see there are several ways to make it happen.

Chapter 6:
Simply Irresistible - How To Create Magnetic Content That Your Audience Will Devour

I endured a lot of trauma, abuse and dysfunction growing up. One thing that developed in me was a ton of self-hatred - in particular for those emotional, needy and vulnerable parts of myself - the little boy inside me in particular.

In this image, I was around 7 years old. How can I look at that boy and think ANY of what happened to him was his fault, or that I should hate him for not being able to protect himself or meet his own needs for love, intimacy, affection, safety, etc.?

Now, as a 43 year old, I have the opportunity to try and integrate with and heal those younger parts of myself and my heart.

I can stop hating (and start loving) that little boy inside me.

So, how does any of this relate to business?

As my business coach says, "Income improvement follows self-improvement."

We cannot outperform our self-image.

If I don't work on my internal "stuff," I won't be as successful as I want to in business ... not to mention life!

Have you found that to be true in your own experience?

If you have a thought, feel free to share in the comments!

Content That Matters

The words you just read are from a short, powerful post I shared on LinkedIn that ended up generating thousands of views, dozens of likes and scores of comments in a very short period of time:

Note how I used a personal story (my childhood abuse) to illustrate a key business lesson (the importance of your mindset and emotional health).

49 Likes · 28 Comments

👍 Like 💬 Comment ➡ Share

📈 **3,028 views** of your post in the feed

Therein lies the lesson of magnetic content - mixing your own personal (and powerful) story with important lessons or tips your audience will benefit from.

In this chapter, we'll walk through the building blocks of what goes into creating compelling, creative content that your audience will find irresistible.

How to Choose Your Topic

Remember The 1 Question Survey? ("What do you want to know more about [BLANK]?")

It's time to put those answers into practice!

Before you set out to create a piece of content, you want to focus on a key problem, pain point or particular goal your ideal audience has *told you* they want help with.

Do *not* go out and guess what you think that might be. Even more, do not go out and *assume* you know what your audience wants.

Instead, ask them.

Once you have enough insight to get a clear idea of what problem your topic should solve or what goal it will help someone reach, then you're ready to create your piece of content.

Write The Headline First

One of the best tricks I learned during my time guest blogging for *Inc. Magazine* was to write my article headline *first,* before I'd ever penned a single piece of copy for the blog post.

Write an irresistible headline *first,* and then, once you have it nailed down, craft the rest of your content to deliver on the headline's promise.

I also remember feeling like my business coach (John Michael Morgan) had slapped me across the face the first time I heard him tell me I should spend 90 percent of my time on a blog post writing the headline, and 10 percent on the actual content of the post itself.

It seemed backward, but it's absolutely true.

Headlines are *that* important. If you can't come up with a great headline that stops someone's online scrolling long enough to ensure he or she taps or clicks onto your post, all is lost before it even begins.

Writing a compelling headline is a skill that improves the more you do it, and it takes a lot of time and practice to master. With that said, there are numerous tools, templates and strategies you can utilize to improve your headline writing in short order.

(Note: I've put together all my favorite headline resources, tools and tips at https://ContentMarketingMachine.com/Bonus)

Two Elements of Successful Headlines

In many cases, an eye-grabbing headline will either promise *utility* (demonstrating how to do something of value or useful) or invoke *curiosity* (make the person reading the headline curious about what's inside).

Here are a few examples from my own blog posts:

Curiosity-Themed Headlines

Why I Cried for 8 Minutes Straight Yesterday

The Greatest Lie Ever Told

That Time My Pants Got Pulled Down in Public

Utility-Themed Headlines

4 DIY Tools for Creating Online Marketing Videos

How to Land New Clients in 14 Seconds or Less

How to Make Your LinkedIn Invites Irresistible!

In addition, the ability to *surprise* someone with a headline that isn't "typical" can work wonders.

"The more unexpected the information, the more [brain] processing time it is given," notes Jonah Sachs in his book *Winning The Story Wars.* "In other words, whether you're hunting on the savannah or choosing between millions of videos on YouTube, your brain is programmed to ignore almost everything and hone in only on what is most important or interesting."

This is why headline writing is more art than science. Finding what pushes those *curiosity* or *utility* buttons with your target audience is where the magic is at!

Warning: Headlines May Vary

Also, I've also found is that the *type* of headline you write depends on the platform you're sharing it on.

For example, I'd argue that the best "headline" (i.e. subject line) for an email is going to be something *conversational*, like "can you believe this?" or "it shocked me."

(I'd also argue for writing these "headlines" in lowercase and not using complete sentences, given that chatty/conversational approaches are the norm with email subject lines.)

Here's why I take this "headline" approach with email: In today's inbox, there's such an overuse and abuse of formal-sounding, business-heavy subject lines and sales offers that the only messages we *urgently* look at are ones that capture our *curiosity.*

Say, for example, I wanted to send you an email about how to use LinkedIn's built-in Search Engine to find your ideal sales leads online.

I could put the subject line as: *"How To Use LinkedIn Search To Find Your Ideal Sales Leads."*

That's straight *utility*, including a promise and a payoff for reading my note. It's not bad, but it also doesn't grab your attention and all but *demand* you open up and read the entire email *right now*, does it?

Now, what if my email subject line read like this: *it shocked me.*

You'd immediately want to know: *What shocked you? What happened?*

Especially if the first line of the email (after the subject line) read like this:

I couldn't believe what I was seeing. In fact, I looked over my shoulder, sure that someone was about to burst into the room and tell me it was a all a big setup.

The email could continue like this:

It couldn't be this easy … could it?

And then I'd pivot into my "shocking" discovery … that you can use LinkedIn's built-in member database like a big search engine, finding your ideal prospects by job title, location and so on.

See how the headline / subject line set the table for this irresistible introduction to the topic of LinkedIn and lead generation? And how the first few lines of the email (which can be seen on most email inbox message previews) build off the intrigue and curiosity of the subject line?

To be clear, this strategy (a conversational and curiosity-invoking tone with your headline) works great for an email, but might not necessarily translate to a blog post or training video you post on YouTube.

With a blog post, perhaps a headline like "The Secret Spot To Find Your Ideal Sales Leads Online" might work better to capture someone's attention by playing on curiosity. Or, perhaps a straight *utility* headline like "The Fast (and Easy) Way To Find Your Ideal Leads using LinkedIn Search" might play well, too.

Whereas on YouTube, where "How To", utility-type videos are among the most searched content on the platform, a headline like "How To Find Sales Leads on LinkedIn" is likely to be much more effective than *"it shocked me."*

With Headlines, Context Matters

Keep in mind too *how* people are going to be consuming your content. Are they typing a search term into YouTube? Or is your email arriving in their inbox because they signed up for one of your lead magnets a few days ago?

In the case of YouTube, since it is the second largest search engine in the world after Google, which now *owns* YouTube, you'll want to format your headline as the answer to a search query.

So "it shocked me" isn't going to cut it. Instead, something like "How To [Blank]" or "The Easy Way To [Blank]" or "Best Way To [Blank]" is going to be much better, since *those* are the terms people type into a search engine when looking for a solution to a problem.

Needless to say, platform-specific strategy should play into your headline choices, meaning that a "one headline fits all" approach to a piece of content is *not* a good idea.

More on Curiosity (and Urgency)

Also, remember this: As human beings, we're wired to stop at *nothing* to satisfy our curiosity. We also have a fear of missing out (FOMO) dynamic in play, which is why phrases such as "Limited Time" or "Limited Spots Available" are such a part of the advertising and marketing lexicon.

Putting a limit or deadline onto something makes people sit up and take notice, because it forces some *urgency* into the equation. Urgency is a powerful tool with headlines, because it forces people to deal with your content *now* as opposed to pushing it to the bottom of an inbox or bookmark list.

Granted, you can't always find legitimate urgency to work into a headline. And, in those cases, *curiosity* works incredibly well.

Another Approach: What's The Benefit?

One other element that can work well in headlines is being *benefit-driven*.

Say you want to lose weight, and you want to do it in a fast, easy and simple fashion.

A *benefit-driven* headline that might catch your attention could look like this:

1 Simple Exercise That Helps You Lose 10 Lbs. in Just 10 Minutes Per Day!

The more enticing benefits you can work into a headline, the better. And, as I mentioned previously, people love *fast, simple and easy.* Your audience will *always* choose to engage with content that promises the least amount of pain or effort to reach their goal or solve their problem.

Headlines Matter. Like, *Really* Matter.

I could write an entire book on creating effective headlines, but let's leave it at this: You *must* find a way to craft compelling headlines that stop someone's scroll long enough to get him or her to tap or click through to consume your content.

Utilize themes like *utility, curiosity, urgency* and *benefits* in your headlines whenever possible, and you'll be well on your way to stopping someone's scroll.

(Reminder: Go to https://ContentMarketingMachine.com/Bonus to get access to all the headline tools, tips and templates I've outlined here.)

How To Structure Your Content

No matter what type of content you are creating (visual, audio or written), there's a specific structure that will ensure you get great engagement from your audience.

It begins with a *hook,* which is the first few lines of written content or the opening to your video, audio or image display.

Remember what I mentioned earlier from *Story Wars: "The more unexpected the information, the more processing time it is given."*

An introduction that stops people in their tracks (meaning it is unique, intriguing, unusual or unexpected in some way) is key.

For example, I began this chapter with a piece of content that started with me sharing a story and photo related to my childhood abuse.

On LinkedIn, in particular, *nobody* is sharing personal content like that, which, in turn, makes people *stop and take notice* in order for their brains to process this "unusual" piece of content that showed up among other posts about business and industry news.

(Note, I'm not doing this to try and trick or manipulate people, but rather to catch their attention long enough to consume my content.)

Remember, that piece of content I created had a strong introductory *hook* (a grainy childhood photo and opening lines about childhood abuse), but it also delivered a valuable business lesson on the importance of your mindset and emotional health as it relates to being successful in business.

(Please note: If your content doesn't actually *deliver* something of value or benefit to your audience, a strong opening hook will be wasted effort.)

Getting Nutty

After your introduction or "hook," you need to quickly pivot into what journalists call the "nut graph" - a short paragraph that quickly explains the value, lesson or benefit that you'll be sharing within the overall piece of content.

Using the earlier example of a blog post on the power and value of video marketing, you could write a nut graph like this:

Given that 70 percent of all online content consumed today is video, and the fact that YouTube is now the second largest search engine on the planet, there's no longer a debate on whether or not having a video presence online matters. With that in mind, let's move into the five simple ways you can immediately begin leveraging online video to generate more sales leads, win new business and boost your brand.

A good "nut graph" sets the stage for the rest of the post, whetting the reader, viewer or listener's appetite for what's to come.

Once you have a solid introduction and nut graph in place, next is the actual "body copy" or "meat" of your post - the tips, training or tools you promised to share. Make sure you deliver on your promise in this section, as it is the *key* to building up the credibility, authority and trust you will need later on to convince someone to give you more time, attention or money based on this piece of content.

Calling All Customers

After delivering the value you promised, you want to finish your post by offering a "Call To Action" (CTA), giving the reader, viewer or listener a next step to take. It could be reading another post, listening to a related podcast episode, subscribing to your YouTube channel, going to your online calendar to book a free discovery call or something else.

The key here is that you *include* a CTA at the end of each piece of content. You never want people to just "walk away" from your blog post, training video, book, podcast or anything else without inviting them further into your sales funnel!

This is why *connecting* your content and stitching together sales funnels built around related pieces of content and topics is critical.

For instance, if you write a short blog on how to improve your LinkedIn profile in order to attract more clients, the CTA might be to download a longer eBook or some training videos that dive deeper into the topic. Next, once someone signs up for that additional content, you deliver it, then pivot them into a related topic - perhaps it's how to find and engage your ideal clients and prospects on LinkedIn.

Finally, you finish up by offering your full online training course or 1-on-1 coaching to help someone *apply* all the content and knowledge you've been sharing for free up to this point.

The Story of All Great Content

Whenever I set out to create a piece of content built around a specific strategy, theme or topic, I always start by asking myself this question:

Do I have a good story for that?

It might be a story from my own personal life (like my childhood abuse story to illustrate the importance of your emotional health and mindset at work) or one I remember from a book, movie or news story.

The key is, you need to have some sort of *story* to tell as part of your content creation.

There is no other way around it. Facts and figures will not suffice. As human beings, we are *horrible* at rote memorization of facts, figures and generic information. Instead, we encode and remember information that comes delivered in the form of a scene or story.

For instance, when you see the image here, what do you think of?

If I did my job at the beginning of this chapter, this image should trigger my story about the importance of emotional health and mindset in being successful. This photo and the scene I painted with words in the post are the encoding mechanism and delivery device for this piece of information.

"To transform static, flat information into something that's dynamic and alive, you'll employ the medium of stories," writes Nancy Duarte in her book *Resonate*. "Stories reshape information into meaning."

"Stories are easy to remember and repeat," she adds. "When you present information in an anecdotal form you add an emotional charge. Stories are also a more digestible format for information."

Even more important, telling a great story makes your audience *feel* something, and the way into someone's wallet is through his or her heart.

"Stories help an audience visualize what you do or what you believe," Duarte writes. "They make others' hearts more pliable. Sharing experiences in the form of a story creates a shared experience and visceral connection. When we listen to a story, the chemicals in our body change and our mind becomes transfixed."

In the realm of sales and marketing, sharing a great *story* about your brand or business has become the gold standard.

"I can think of a lot of people who balk at big promises. I can think of plenty more who couldn't care less about a bulleted list of shocking statistics. But, I can't think of a single person who can resist a good story. Can you?" ask Michael Masterson and John Forde in their book, *Great Leads: The Six Easiest Ways To Start Any Sales Message*.

"Everybody loves a good story," they continue. "As a way to communicate, nothing feels more natural. So, doesn't it make sense that when someone says, 'Let me tell you a story …' you perk up and listen?"

Getting Personal

Carrying forward the example piece of content I started this chapter with, telling a *personal* story with your content is one of the most powerful strategies you can utilize.

"If you're like many professionals, using stories to create emotional appeal feels unnatural because it requires showing at least some degree of vulnerability to people you don't personally know all that well," Duarte writes in *Resonate*. "Telling a personal story can be especially daunting, because great personal stories have a conflict or complication that exposes your humanness or flaws.

"But these are also the stories that have the most inherent power to change others. People enjoy following a leader who has survived personal challenges and can share her narrative of struggle and victory (or defeat) comfortably.

"Stories link one person's heart to another," she continues. "Values, beliefs, and norms become intertwined. When this happens, your idea can more readily manifest as reality in their minds."

Your Audience = The Hero

Another important element to remember in crafting story-themed content is making sure it's not all about you.

Instead, especially with longer-form content, you must quickly pivot from your own personal journey or struggle and make the journey about your reader, viewer or listener accomplishing his or her goals.

"Whether you're trying to connect with your audience through stories or some other way, you must remember that your presentation isn't all about you," Duarte writes in *Resonate*. "Begin the presentation from a shared place of understanding. Make it about the audience."

You = Yoda / Your Customer = Luke Skywalker

The most well-known example of this approach (making your customer the Hero of a story) plays out in what Joseph Campbell calls "The Hero's Journey."

Made famous from movies like the original *Star Wars* trilogy, The Hero's Journey takes an otherwise normal, everyday person (think of Luke Skywalker from the original *Star Wars* movies) on a journey where he or she is called out of a mundane life and up into a larger, much more dangerous, life-and-death adventure.

A critical role in The Hero's Journey involves a *guide* or *mentor* showing up early on in the story to help our hero begin transforming from that everyday, regular Joe or Jane into someone special - his or her true (and heroic) self.

One of the most celebrated mentors in pop culture is Yoda from the *Star Wars* movies. The little green Jedi is the character most directly responsible for transforming Luke Skywalker from orphaned farm kid into the Hero of the Universe.

In the case of *your* content and the journey you want to take your audience on, your role is to be Yoda.

Great content not only shows someone how *you* achieved a goal or overcame a problem, but it also inspires the reader/listener/viewer to believe he or she *can do it, too.*

You will serve as his or her guide, bringing him or her the tools, tips and techniques needed to achieve a specific goal or overcome a specific challenge.

And, if you share your own personal story and journey in the context of doing this, your reader/listener/viewer will feel comfortable enough to trust you can help him or her achieve it, too, because you were once in his or her shoes.

It is critical that you share your own humble beginnings when crafting a piece of content that is meant to inspire your audience to achieve a goal or solve a problem. If you place yourself as a guru who has never struggled and who achieved instant success in your area of expertise, people will not relate to you.

Even worse, they will think, "Well, sure *you* made it, but you're you. I could never do the same thing."

Instead, you want people to realize that you were once just like them, struggling with the same challenges and problems, and that, once you found your solution / strategy / system and applied it, everything changed, and you reached the goal or solved the problem. And now, you want to show them how to do the same thing!

That is what great content does - it places you as the time-tested, battle-proven guide who has walked in the very same shoes and situations as your audience … and who emerged victorious.

The Role of Emotion is Key

A natural byproduct of telling a great story is that your audience will *feel* something as a result of consuming your content.

Provoking an emotional response with your content is critical if you want to generate a meaningful outcome for your business.

Remember my story earlier about *Feed My Starving Children* and the power of the content shared in that video about how *my* volunteering and donations could feed children on the other side of the earth?

The content in that video stirred emotions deep inside me, and, *while I was emotional, I was also ready to buy.* In this case, it meant donating money on the spot to *Feed My Starving Children.*

As I mentioned earlier in the book, *we buy based on emotion.*

"Stimulate your audience through appeals to their feelings of pain or pleasure," Duarte shares in *Resonate.* "When people feel these emotions, they will throw reason out the window; *people make important decisions based on emotion.*"

So it only follows that your content needs to invoke emotion, to make your audience *feel* something.

Maybe it's inspiration, or motivation, or a sense of helping someone in need.

Maybe it's just a good laugh and a sense of warmth toward the person creating and sharing the content.

All of it is important, because an audience that *feels* is an audience that *buys*.

"Your enthusiasm is contagious," a new customer told me after watching my LinkedIn Riches webinar and purchasing the online course. "And I loved your sense of humor. I knew I'd enjoy learning from you."

How To Invoke Emotion With Your Content

Depending on the type of content you're creating, there are different ways to generate an emotional response from your audience.

With the written word (books, blogs, etc.), telling a compelling story will work best. Authentic images (think of the shot of me as a 7 year old boy) can also evoke an emotional response in a powerful fashion.

With audio and video content, your communication style (tone of voice, facial expressions, etc.) and personality (humor, enthusiasm, etc.) are the keys to making sure your audience *feels* something.

The biggest sin in marketing (and content creation) is to be boring.

So don't be!

It's important to note that you don't have to invent a new personality or approach to ensure your content has an emotional impact. In fact, we'll spend the next chapter walking through exactly how *you* are already perfectly positioned to stand out in the crowded content marketplace!

Chapter 7:
The Secret Sauce Nobody Else Can Replicate

Okay here it goes ... *I'm not perfect.*

I was abused as a young boy. I take medication for depression and anxiety. I often struggle with shame and self-hatred.

And when I disclose this to clients and customers ... it often leads to some of the highest quality, longest-lasting and most lucrative business relationships I've ever had.

Here's why: When I risk *the right amount* of vulnerability, transparency and honesty in creating and sharing content with potential clients and prospects, it offers up an important opportunity to bond that goes beyond just doing business together.

And the same is true for you.

The more you insert yourself (the *real* you - your authentic personality, your vulnerabilities and challenges, etc.) into the content you create, the more engagement, success and business you'll generate as a result.

This is the secret sauce that nobody else on the planet can replicate.

Simply put, there is only one *you.*

And, the more you put yourself into the content you create and share with your ideal audience, the more people will get to *know, like and trust* you … and want to do business with you as a result.

Transparency vs. Too Much

Notice I said "the right amount" of personal sharing. Because if you turn a piece of content into an episode of *Oprah* or *Dr. Phil,* cutting open a vein about your life issues, you will turn people off in a hurry and scare them away. I always try to err on the side of being honest or vulnerable without being dramatic or going into gory detail.

Also, it doesn't have to be heavy issues. For example, since I work from home, I'm often in the midst of madness with our three young boys and Rosie the dog running around. My biggest client called one time a few years back and started the conversion with, "What are you up to right now, John?"

"Well, I'm sitting at the kitchen table helping my five-year-old write a story about a talking penguin for his homework assignment," I said, laughing. "You asked what I was doing right now, so…"

Now, I knew this client had a couple of young kids, so he could relate to exactly what I was talking about. I probably wouldn't have said the same thing to a client with no family or young kids, but you get the idea.

The other reason for putting the "real" you into the content you create is that *people need a narrative* to attach to you. They need to know your story - who you are, what life experiences helped to shape the person you've become and so on.

As I mentioned in the previous chapter, *story* is how we remember and encode information. Once people know your *story*, they'll never forget who you are, what you do and why you do it.

Finally, sharing your true, authentic self inside the content you create will *attract* the type of people who you'd *want* to do business with - people who enjoy your personality, your style of communicating, who share similar life experiences and therefore feel more "bonded" to you and your story than that of a competitor.

Hiding vs. Honesty

In today's social media-crazed environment, it's easier than ever to hide your flaws and present the perfect and polished version of yourself to the professional world.

I don't know about you, but I've only run across one truly perfect person in all of humanity ... and they nailed Him to a cross 2,000+ years ago. (Yes, I'm a huge fan of Jesus ... more transparency leaking out of me!)

The truth is, none of us are perfect and all of us need encouragement, affirmation and love more than we'd care to admit. We also tend to trust people more who don't pretend to be perfect.

So when you infuse your content with personal stories of your own humanity, people respect you more, not less.

Again, it doesn't have to be heavy issues. It can be your passion for parenting, and how that ties into a business lesson you want to share with your audience. Perhaps a funny story about your kids reminded you of an important principle related to negotiating business deals.

You don't have to go out and climb a mountain or skydive - just reflect on your own life journey and stories or lessons learned that can be sprinkled into and tied to the major themes of content you create.

Relational vs. Transactional

Here's why this matters so much: I have no problem switching cell phone providers if I can get a better deal. The reason is that I have *no human relationship* with my cell phone provider, and (more important) they don't even try to build any type of meaningful relationship with me.

Now, ask me to stop doing business with someone who I've *personally* known, liked and trusted for years, and I'm much less likely to switch - even if you are offering me a lower price or better deal.

The Point of Getting Personal

And, at the end of the day, nobody wants to do business with a stranger, do they?

Instead, we always want to do business with people we *know, like and trust.*

This happens all the time in real life, and we don't even realize it.

For instance, we recently had a contractor come to our home for a bid on some landscaping.

After he left, my wife said, "I like him. He's like us - he has three young boys, he played hockey growing up, so I feel like you and him will get along well."

Notice how my wife didn't start with the bottom line (his price), but rather the *relational* aspect of our interaction. Sure, price can be a huge factor, but it wouldn't have mattered how cheap the guy's bid was if the *personal* factor didn't get addressed first.

The same is true of our interactions with others online - you're going to first tap into the *relational* part of your brain when figuring out who you'd like to work with. You're going to look for someone whose *content* demonstrates to you that this is a person you can get to know, like and trust. Someone you'll enjoy working with, someone who "gets" you and what you're trying to accomplish. Someone who is being real and authentic, who isn't posing or pretending.

And the more personal or relationship-based the project might be (such as Business Coaching, Consulting, Branding or Marketing, Investing, Legal Services, etc.), the more important *knowing, liking and trusting* the person providing the service becomes, doesn't it?

What To Avoid

When you create content, don't infuse it with political or religious rants, because all that will do is alienate and annoy your audience.

Now, in my case, I *do* create and share content that talks about Jesus Christ, but I'm careful *not* to share it in a way that comes across as "holier than thou" or fire and brimstone. Instead, I always try and lead with my own brokenness and need for a savior. I've found it's hard for someone to criticize me when I'm openly admitting what a mess I am and how badly I need a hero and savior to rescue, heal and love me.

Now, because Jesus is such a big passion of mine, I can't help but let that leak out into some of my content. Also, I've made a personal decision in my life and business that I'm okay losing potential clients and customers over posts about Jesus.

What I'm *not* okay with is losing potential customers over my political views, so I try to avoid political posts like the plague.

With all that said, remember that it's best not to talk religion or politics at the dinner table - or online. So focus instead on creating content that shares more about who you are - your life, your family, your personal and professional journey, life lessons learned, etc.

How To Integrate Yourself into Your Content

As I mentioned earlier, the key is finding a way to tie together the *personal* and *professional* whenever you set out to create a piece of content. For example, I always start my content creation efforts by trying to think of a *personal story* that will illustrate the *business lesson* I want to share.

As an illustration, a few years ago I wanted to write a blog post about the importance of taking action and not relying on others to dictate the level of happiness and success you can achieve in your life and career.

(This was in support of one of my other books, *Fired Up!*, which you can learn more about online at www.FiredUpLive.com.)

So, instead of just stating those principles as part of the blog post, I found a way to encode and deliver those business lessons inside of a personal story.

Here's how it looked:

How a Game of Touch Football Changed My Career Forever

When I was in seventh grade, the big thing to do at recess was play touch football on the blacktop of our school's massive parking lot.

There was just one problem – the "cool" kids in my class ran the game, and I wasn't part of their clique. For weeks, I was relegated to the sidelines, watching and wishing that *just once* I'd get invited to play in their game. I was too shy and passive to insert myself into the game or demand a spot, so I stood there and watched.

And all my wishing and hoping didn't change a thing.

You know what did? *Taking action.*

One day, I brought my own football to school, and I invited some of the other kids languishing on the sidelines to go off and start our own game. It sounds easy, but trust me, in the social jungle of seventh grade boys, it was a gutsy move, one that required enormous risk on my part.

As I feared, many of my friends flat out refused or rebuffed my offer. I was part of a group of boys a notch below the "cool" kids. We were decent athletes, we were smart, but we weren't part of the elite social group in our grade.

Now, we *were* above the nerds, misfits and dorks, but not by much. (I realize it's not politically correct or sensitive to refer to my grade school contemporaries with those terms, but that's how we classified kids in seventh grade during the late 1980s.) The best analogy I can give is that we were card-carrying members of the middle class in the St. Rose of Lima social jungle's pecking order.

When it came to my new playground football venture, this left me with one choice – *invite the dorks*. It was a form of social suicide, but I did it anyway.

Making a Way

I was tired of standing on the sidelines. I was tired of waiting, watching and hoping. I was tired of being passive, resigned to having others write the script of my seventh grade social standing and recess time.

So I took my football and a handful of dorks and started my own game.

Everyone from the "cool" game laughed at us. We were mocked. One of my friends in the middle class group referred to my new venture as "the JV game" or "Nemo and the 'B' team."

Remember, this was seventh grade. Boys at that age can be cruel and cutting. (I won't even mention how catty the girls can be!) All of us were looking for our place in the pack. In no arena does this type of masculine testing and measuring show up more than the athletic one.

My new football game *was* horrible. The nerds and dorks couldn't catch a pass, and some of them didn't even know the rules of touch football.

It was awful quality. Embarrassing, even.

You know what else it was?

Fun.

I was the star of my new league, firing passes that bounced off the hands of kids with thick glasses and retainers. I directed an offense of clumsy boys running bow-legged pass routes that I drew up on my open palm inside the huddle.

I didn't belittle anyone. Instead, I encouraged them. I pumped their tires. I fired them up.

On that playground, I became my favorite quarterback, the Denver Broncos' John Elway. I scrambled. I passed. I swaggered. I led game-winning drives. I talked trash.

I loved every second of it. The other kids did too. We *played.* We had fun.

Then something funny happened.

After a few weeks, some of my friends from the middle class group wandered over. At first, they just watched, making snarky comments from the sidelines about how bad the quality of the game was.

"Why don't you shut up and play with us, then?" I'd yell back. "Quit standing there and get in the game!"

They eventually did, worrying less about what the "cool" kids thought and joining what was still called "Nemo's 'B' team" or "the JV game."

To this day, those seventh grade football games are some of the happiest memories I have.

Change the Game

I need to ask you: *Are you standing on the sidelines of life right now? Are you stuck inside the bowels of some massive corporation, toiling away in a cubicle and wishing for something more? Are you struggling to find meaning, passion and purpose in your career?*

If so, what are you going to *do* about it?

A few years ago, bored and unhappy at my day job, I drove home every evening fantasizing about the day I'd quit.

But dreaming never changed my situation.

Taking massive action did. Developing an exit strategy, starting up side projects, networking, learning, seeking advice from others who were doing what I wanted to step into ... that's what moved me off the sidelines and into the game.

No Risk, No Reward

In any great story, a character must *risk* something to advance toward his or her goal.

Your life is no different. In order to get the career you want, doing the work you love, you're going to have to risk something of significance to get there.

So let's get to it: Where are you holding back in your life and career right now? What aren't you chasing after? What haunts you in those quiet moments of the early morning, before the chaos of the day distracts you and keeps your heart and head occupied? Where have you been afraid to go?

I want you to say out loud what your biggest fear is. Or write it down. I want you to put out into the light of day *the worst possible thing* that might happen if you start taking the type of risks I'm talking about.

Is it being embarrassed in front of your peers on the playground? Is it losing the approval of your parents, who think your passion for poetry or music is a pipe dream and that you need to get a "real" job? Is it not being able to pay the mortgage or feed your children? Is it as simple as the fear of falling on your face and having the Twitter hashtag #Fail attached to your business or life?

It's important, because I'm going to let you in on a little secret: *Nobody remembers you for the times you've tried and failed. Unless you stay there.*

"Every strike gets me closer to the next home run," baseball legend Babe Ruth used to say. Ruth struck out 1,330 times in his career. He also hit 714 home runs. What's he more remembered for?

Thomas Edison invented the light bulb, the phonograph and the motion picture camera. He also had countless inventions that did *not* work or change society.

"I have not failed," he said. "I've just found ten thousands ways that won't work."

Edison understood: You can't get from here to there without risking something significant. He also understood that failure was both inevitable and even encouraging.

Let me leave you with this – what are you risking by *not* taking any action today?

If it helps, leave a comment below or send me a message and tell me just one simple action you are going to take right here, right now, *today,* to move one step closer to the life you want and work you love.

See you on the playground!

(Note: You can read more stories like that one in my book *Fired Up!* - go online to www.FiredUpLive.com for more info.)

Mixing it Together

That post blended business with a personal story, and re-reading it, I *wish* I was always that brave and strong and confident-sounding in my life and business.

But that's the point, isn't it?

Being real, being human, sharing our struggles and successes … *that* is the foundation of deep, powerful and important relationships. The more you can tap into building that foundation by inserting your personality into your content, the better.

What Works Well

Depending on the *type* of content and the platform you're sharing it on, certain types of "personal" or personality-driven posts work better.

For instance, if you're looking to just fire off a quick status update on a network like Facebook or LinkedIn, a shorter amount of text along with a photo works best - especially a "behind the scenes" look at your work life, or perhaps a quick snapshot of your family life or favorite pet makes sense.

You'd be wise not to ignore these small and seemingly insignificant posts, because each one helps build your *personal brand* online, keeping you in front of people while also helping them get to know, like and trust you a bit more.

For a longer-form blog post, video or podcast, you can get more in-depth and personal, starting with a powerful personal story that makes the audience emotional and curious to find out what happened next.

Don't Overdo It

Let me be clear: I'm not saying every single piece of content you create and share *has* to have something personal in it.

For example, I might share a "personal" type status update on LinkedIn (where I spend most of my time online generating leads) maybe 2-3 times a week. Now, I post 3-5 status updates *daily* on LinkedIn, but most are business-driven pieces of news, content or offers to a lead magnet on my website.

I don't spend all day, every day, hammering my LinkedIn news feed with dog photos, personal stories or tales of my latest vacation. Instead, I look to sprinkle in the personal when it makes sense and feels natural with these shorter, quick status update type posts.

Also, sometimes I don't have a good *personal* story, so I borrow one - like I did in citing Thomas Edison on failure or Babe Ruth on striking out and hitting home runs in the blog post about touch football.

Get Out of Your Comfort Zone

I can hear the cynics from here - "Listen, Nemo, this is *business* we're talking about. Nobody really wants to hear *my* story ... I'm not that interesting, anyway!"

If you're having those types of thoughts right now, feel free to smack yourself in the face. Those are lies, because, in reality *everyone* is interesting.

You are the only version of *you* this world has ever known! You have a unique life, a unique story and a unique personality to offer this world.

Whatever you've been through to this point, sharing some part of your story that *also* ties into the type of business lesson or strategy you want to share is an ideal way to engage your audience with content.

Make Sure You Resonate

"There's truth in the cliché, 'Just be yourself,' Nancy Duarte writes in *Resonate*. "Showing your humanness when you present is a great way to stand out. It's a quality that's totally lacking in most presentations today - even though the entire audience consists of humans! What people are really looking for when they sit down at a presentation is some kind of human connection.

"Being true to yourself involves showing and sharing emotion. The spirit that motivates most great storytellers is 'I want you to feel what I feel,' and the effective narrative is designed to make this happen. That's how the information is bound to the experience and rendered unforgettable."

Preach, Nancy, preach!

She continues: "Even with mountains of facts, you can still fail to resonate. That's because resonance doesn't come from the information itself, but rather from the *emotional impact* of that information. This doesn't mean that you should abandon facts entirely. Use plenty of facts, but accompany them with emotional appeal.

"Personal stories are an important part of most great presentations. There will be times in your presentation when you want your audience to feel a specific emotion. One way to do this is to talk about a time when you felt that very same emotion. This technique establishes a connection between you and the audience that's sincere and credible. A catalog of personal stories related to various emotions can be a helpful resource."

In one of her TED talks on giving great presentations, Nancy Duarte gets personal, sharing about her own brokenness and abusive childhood and how it shaped her story and how others can find purpose out of pain.

(Note: You can find her TED Talk via this link: https://www.ted.com/talks/ nancy_duarte_the_secret_structure_of_great_talks)

A Personal Question

Let me ask you: How badly do you want to succeed?

Actually, here's a better question - how badly do you want to have an impact professionally and personally?

What drives you? What makes you tick?

For most people, once you get below the surface items like fame, money, success, etc., it typically involves *significance* - to know that you matter. That, if you get hit by a bus tomorrow, people will have something to say about you beyond, "Man, he sure was good with a spreadsheet."

Inserting *yourself* into your content is that chance. Beyond being a smart business and lead generation strategy, sharing yourself in the ways I'm talking about in this chapter moves you beyond the mundane and into a place where you can actually impact people's lives in a significant way!

I'm not talking about you needing to be the next Gandhi or Martin Luther King Jr., but just being *human*, having the type of impact and influence on others that deep down you know you were *born* to do!

So it's time to get *real* with your content. Find ways to share your struggles and successes in a way that invites your audience into a deeper relationship.

And *always* tie it into a larger theme, strategy or lesson. Because every great story (even your most personal ones!) have one.

Just today, I got an email from someone who purchased my LinkedIn Riches Online Course in hopes of growing a nonprofit organization birthed out of a personal story (domestic violence and abuse).

It's a heavy topic, but one, as the person explained in her note, where she wants to utilize that pain for a larger purpose. The person is writing a book and has a story to tell, one that is harrowing and horrible at times, but also filled with hope, inspiration and an impact that can help countless others who have gone through something similar.

My friend, never underestimate what it is that you (and only you!) have to say and share inside of the content you create.

Let us into your life, and we'll become your friends, fans and followers.

Chapter 8:
You Have To See It To Believe It

T he man tried to slip in unnoticed, sneaking in a side door as I stood at the front of a hotel ballroom giving a presentation on using LinkedIn for lead generation.

"Hey, everybody, let's welcome our new friend!" I shouted into the microphone as heads turned to see the latecomer walking into the room. "Just so you know, I'm *killing it* up here. You made a great decision to come, buddy."

The crowd roared, and I was off and running, jumping back into the presentation.

When it comes to creating and sharing content, the most powerful and engaging form comes by being face-to-face with the people you want to purchase your products or services.

But, aside from public speaking or 1-on-1 coffee meetings where you speak directly to your prospects in the same room, what types of "content" work best to engage (and persuade) your audience to do business with you?

Video Killed The Radio Star

One of the reasons face-to-face interactions work so well to sell your products and services is that people get to *see* you - your facial expressions, your body language, your smile, etc.

As human beings, we need to feel *connected* to someone before we can know, like or trust him or her.

Utilizing online video and being on camera is a fast, easy and effective way to build that critical connection with your audience. People not only hear your voice (which is uniquely you), they also see your facial expressions, feel your emotion coming through the camera, and look into your eyes to decide if they trust you or not.

Today, you don't need a TV studio, expensive equipment or an enormous advertising budget to become a video star. YouTube is living proof of that, as otherwise unknown people become (seemingly) overnight superstars thanks to viral videos, often done with little more than an iPhone and a friend giggling behind the camera.

If you pay attention to the video stars of YouTube, you'll notice they usually build their audiences around a shared passion or subject, such as playing video games, parenting, cooking and so on.

The reason someone becomes a YouTube star is that his or her video content resonates and builds camaraderie with an audience of like-minded individuals. And, even though anyone with a smartphone and Internet connection can create online video, there's still something unique about seeing someone speaking with confidence, humor or passion on camera. It adds an additional layer of credibility and authority, especially if the person on camera has an engaging presence and personality.

Video is Ubiquitous

As of this writing, I've seen studies that claim 70 percent or more of all content consumed online today is video, and that the number is only expected to climb. YouTube is now the second largest search engine in the world. And, since Google *owns* YouTube, those videos now display in Google searches as well.

If you want to know how to change a flat tire on the exact make and model of your car, there's a good chance someone already made a YouTube video showing you how it works. The same is true with yard projects, software demonstrations, recipes or anything else you can show someone else how to do in real life.

Thanks to handheld smartphones, data plans and nonstop connectivity, video is indeed taking over the Internet. This presents an enormous opportunity for you as a content creator to build a passionate (and powerful) audience of subscribers and viewers.

Types of Video Content

With all that in mind, you still need to create quality (and compelling) video content if you want it to engage your ideal audience online.

There are several different ways to do that, including being "on camera" speaking directly to your audience, interviewing someone else via Skype or other video chat software, being "behind" the camera and demonstrating something on your computer screen or narrating over webinar slides or stock video clips.

Having people "see" your face on camera is the best way to quickly build the *know, like and trust* elements with an audience. The more video you do, the more people get comfortable "seeing" you on a regular basis, and in fact will look forward to your latest "show" or clip that you share online.

If you're not comfortable on camera, that's fine too. I make almost all my videos "behind" the camera, instead talking into a microphone while showing something on my screen (like a lead generation technique you can utilize on LinkedIn) or speaking while showing stock video clips or slides to illustrate a point.

Video Content Ideas

So what goes into a good video? How long should it be?

These are all valid questions, and the answer is … it depends.

Before you sit down to create a video, you need to know the strategy and goal behind it.

For instance, if you want to shoot a quick, "Day in the Life" iPhone video of you attending a cool conference in a beautiful location, that's fast and easy, and the goal should be to build your personal brand and remind people about one of your professional passions. You'll likely see a lot of views and engagement, especially if the video is quick, short and showcasing a gorgeous outdoor setting, but it's unlikely to lead to any immediate business opportunities.

Whereas, if you're doing a more in-depth tutorial on a computer screen of how to utilize Facebook Ads, you can expect fewer views and less engagement, but those who *do* watch and engage are much more likely to reach out wanting more, leading to more meaningful business discussions.

Both approaches are valuable, and, at the end of the day, with limited time and resources, you just need to decide what type of video marketing (if any) will move the needle for you and your business.

For me, long-form videos like automated webinars are core to selling my online courses. These webinar videos are time-consuming to create and produce, but they result in ongoing, high-ticket sales over a long period of time.

Outside of that, I might post a "day in the life" video a few times a month on LinkedIn or another platform and tie it to a business or lifestyle lesson, like how

I love the freedom of working from home because it gives me a chance to take my boys sledding in the middle of a snowy day here in Minnesota.

Beyond that, I also create and share "How To" videos a few times a month on things like generating leads with LinkedIn using a certain part of the platform.

Creating Binge-Worthy Content

What's been interesting to me is the "binge" factor with having a YouTube channel stocked with a few dozen of those "How To" videos. For example, I've had multiple people in recent months purchase my LinkedIn Riches Online Course after telling me, "I was searching on YouTube for LinkedIn tips, found one of your videos, loved it, started watching more of them, then eventually got on your webinar and bought the course."

I *love* the long-tail nature of "discoverable" YouTube videos, and have seen my "How To" type videos work best for bringing in leads this way. Again, if you think about how people utilize search engines, they almost always type in some sort of phrase like "how to get XYZ" or "how to [blank] with [blank]," making a video with a "How To" title work well for getting "found" online via search engines.

Motivate. Inspire. Entertain.

If you are going to be on camera, then make sure you inject lots of personality and emotion into your delivery.

Remember the "info-tainment" factor - you must inform *and* entertain people while delivering your content.

Video is a natural medium for this, showcasing your charisma and personality *while* you deliver valuable insights and information.

Speaking with passion and enthusiasm on camera is critical. After all, if *you* don't seem excited about the content you're delivering on camera, why should your audience be?

My favorite comment online with any piece of content is this: "Wow, John, your enthusiasm is contagious. I feel inspired!"

Remember, when your content makes people emotional, when they *feel* something, *that* is when they're ready to buy.

The Overriding Principle = Deliver Value!

No matter what form you decide to utilize with your video content, you *always* want to focus on delivering something of value to your audience.

For a YouTube creator who just wants more views so he or she can court advertisers, perhaps the "value" is being funny or entertaining.

For those of us in business, it might mean showing someone how to get a quick win using a specific strategy or technique we can show them via video.

Either way, remember, people want to be entertained *and* informed. Keep the *info-tainment* principle top of mind when creating video content, and you'll do well.

(To see a sampling of my most successful and highest-converting video content, go to https://ContentMarketingMachine.com/Bonus)

Views vs. Results

I'll talk more about this later in the book, but don't get caught up with how many views, shares or comments your online videos receive.

Here's why: The last time I checked, you still cannot deposit likes, comments or views into your bank account.

Always and forever, the best metric to measure your content by is this: Does it directly or indirectly result in people paying you for a product or service? If so, that's a valuable piece of content.

In my experience, people get *way* too hung up on all the features and metrics of online videos or other forms of content, obsessing over those numbers instead of dissecting whether or not the content actually leads to any meaningful business or lead generation.

Chapter 9:
Can We Talk? Listen To This Advice

With all the talk about video, it can be easy to forget the passive (and powerful) nature of audio content.

Each week, for example, your voice can *literally* be in the heads of hundreds (or even) thousands of people around the world thanks to a weekly podcast. And, next to "seeing" someone face-to-face or via video, nothing is more powerful than someone hearing your voice (with its unique tone, inflection and sound) inside his or her head for minutes (or even hours) at a time.

Audio on the Go

The advent of iPhones and other "smart" devices has made it easy for people to take audio wherever they go - from mowing the lawn to riding the bus to walking the dog.

As a result, Podcasts, which first came into existence in the early 2000s, have enjoyed a massive renaissance in recent years, growing more and more popular thanks to the ease of access and the binge-worthy nature of episodic shows like *Serial* and others.

So, how can you parlay the popularity of Podcasting into your content marketing strategy?

A former U.S. Army service member has some insights and a story you'll want to pay attention to.

Are You Ready to Ignite? How This Entrepreneur Caught Fire

Stuck in commuter traffic, his cash tapped out from buying and listening to countless audiobooks while driving, John Lee Dumas one day stumbled onto the power of podcasting.

"I just immediately fell in love with the medium," he told me in an interview for my Podcast (Nemo Radio). "I remember thinking, 'This is amazing – on demand, targeted, free content that I can just listen to when I want to and where I want to!'"

Dumas, who spent seven years in the U.S. Army and later tried to find his niche in the professional world, only to, as he put it, "feel like I was dying a slow death in the cubicle," had an awakening during one of those long commutes.

"I started to see, there was this void in the marketplace for a daily, business-themed podcast," he says. "I, personally, as a consumer, wanted to be listening to a podcast every single day that was telling me the story of an inspiring entrepreneur. I wanted that daily motivation, inspiration and lessons for my own life and work."

So, in September 2012, he quit his day job and launched "Entrepreneur On Fire," a daily business podcast. He had no audience, no broadcasting experience, no budget and no sponsors.

Four years and 1,400 episodes later, Dumas now oversees a thriving, 7-figure lifestyle business that generates more than $300,000 per month in revenue.

(Note: You can listen to the entire interview at https://linkedinriches.com/create-army-loyal-podcast-listeners/)

The first six months, Dumas says, were a grind. He was churning out an episode a day, seven days a week, every single week, and had zero income or revenue to show for it.

The tipping point came in Month 7, when a company that acted as an intermediary between advertisers and successful podcasts approached Dumas, asking him if he'd be open to taking on paid sponsors.

A week later, he received his first monetary revenue from "Entrepreneur On Fire" (EOF) in the form of $12,000 in sponsorships.

More importantly, Dumas says, he was building an audience that, in his words, "was beginning to know, like and trust me."

By putting out consistent, free and valuable content every single day, Dumas built a rabid following he affectionately terms "Fire Nation."

"I had opened up this great, two-way form of communication," he says. "And as I started talking to listeners, thanking them for listening to the show, I was also asking what their biggest problems, pain points and challenges were."

Dumas even created a listener avatar he nicknamed "Jimmy," utilizing his vision of the "perfect EOF listener" to guide his content and guest choices for the podcast.

A Trusted Voice + Monetary Solutions

"I became a trusted source for my audience, and I had listened to what they wanted," he says. "So I was ready, eventually, to provide them a solution in the form of products, services and communities when the time was right."

It started with Podcasters' Paradise, an online training program and community Dumas created that has 2,800 members worldwide and has generated more than $3.5 million in sales to date.

That was followed up by a Webinar On Fire online training program and then a new goal-setting guide, The Freedom Journal, which Dumas launched via Kickstarter, raising more than $453,000 and becoming one of the most successful campaigns in the platform's history.

Today, with more than 1 million unique listens per month, "Entrepreneur On Fire" (EOF) is one of the most popular podcasts in the world.

So much so, Dumas shared, that international business icon and motivational speaker Tony Robbins actually had *his* team reach out to Dumas to ask if he'd consider featuring Robbins as a guest on EOF.

"It was surreal," Dumas says. "Here I was, back in 2012, starting with no audience, no revenue, nothing, and now Tony Robbins' team is reaching out asking me if he can appear my show. It's been an incredible ride."

The Power of Podcasting

Another person I spoke with about the power of Podcasts is Cliff Ravenscraft, also known online as *The Podcast Answer Man.*

The reason Podcasts are so effective at engaging your ideal audience is that they are *passive,* meaning your listener can be doing something else (folding laundry, riding a bike, walking the dog, driving to work, etc.) while listening to your wisdom.

Podcasts are also *on demand,* meaning you listen when you *want* to, and when it's convenient for you, Ravenscraft says.

"With podcasting, there's no screen time required," he adds. "Nobody is appearing in your social media feed and distracting or interrupting you with a video or message."

Also, the engagement and attention level of a podcast listener is much more intimate, intense and ultimately valuable, according to Ravenscraft.

"In most cases, people are not just randomly coming across your podcast and listening to it," he says. "Where the real power is, is when somebody has found your content, and he or she liked it, and has clicked the 'Subscribe' button.

"When *that* happens, a majority of the people who find you, who go through all that trouble to search for and subscribe to your show, will listen to *every single episode* you produce. They will hear every syllable of every word you speak every time you put an episode out."

A 2017 study by Edison Research bears that theory out.

Of the 142 million Americans who listened to a podcast in 2017, 85 percent of listeners say they listened to all (or most) of an episode.

With that in mind, if you do a 60 minute podcast each week, your most engaged listeners literally have your voice in their head 52 hours a year, Ravenscraft says.

"Do you think you have any influence in their lives as a result?" he asks.

Audio Content That Engages

When it comes to using Podcasts to win new business, Ravenscraft says you *must* deliver real, legitimate value and content to your ideal audience.

"The stuff that people are paying you for in your coaching calls, the information people are paying you for in your books, put it out there for free in your audio podcast," he says. "Do it consistently, on a week-by-week basis, for free.

"If you give people an opportunity to hear your voice, week after week, while they're driving to work, walking the dog, whatever it is … that convenience, plus the ability to be focused on what you are telling them, is invaluable."

Once you build your audience, you can monetize your show by driving listeners to landing pages for additional training and product sales, inviting them to real-life events or conferences, utilizing ads or sponsorships, and so on.

Listen. Go. Repeat.

As I mentioned earlier, thanks to the iPhone and podcasting apps, access to and interest in podcasts is at an all-time high. Edison's 2017 study revealed that 67 million Americans listen to podcasts monthly, up 14 percent from 2016.

Today, 24 percent of Americans age 12 or older listen to podcasts monthly. For context, 21 percent of Americans are Catholic. Thus, podcast listening is more common than Catholicism in the United States.

"Podcasting today is certainly much easier than it was in [the early 2000s]," Ravenscraft says. "But it's still about finding that percentage of your audience who, after hearing your voice, your passion and your communication style, *love* listening to you and can't wait to hear more."

(NOTE: You can listen to my full interview with Cliff online at https://linkedinriches.com/Cliff/)

Get Inspired. Share Your Story.

The style and format of *your* Podcast is limited only by your creativity and preferred communication style.

Some shows follow a specific format, always featuring certain sections or interview blocks so that listeners know what to expect.

Rather than trying to copy someone else's approach, however, I'm more a fan of doing *you* - leveraging *your* unique style of speaking, structuring and communicating via a Podcast instead.

If you want to go all out and have tons of audio effects, special voiceover actors and dramatic instrumentals between sections of the show, go for it. If you want to build the entire show around expert interviews, make it happen. Or, if you want a raw, stripped down podcast that's just your voice and a powerful story, anecdote or lesson that needs sharing, then do it.

The key is to *do it,* and to (as I've mentioned before) let the marketplace dictate the results.

Who Are You Talking To?

One piece of advice I've found helpful in creating podcasts is to speak as if you're talking to just one person, saying "you" instead of "you guys" or "everyone" or something similar. Remember, your Podcast is typically being listened to by one person individually, so make it feel intimate and personal, like a 1-on-1 coffee meeting or conversation.

You can also build audience loyalty and spread word virally about the podcast by featuring members of your audience on the show. As one example, there are lots of software plugins online that make it easy for listeners to submit voice questions that you can answer on your show.

Going back to the 1 Question Survey, you can ask people to email or submit voice questions answering, *"What do you want to know more about [Blank]?"*

Turn those answers into show topics, and you'll ensure you're hitting on the key issues, pain points and problems your ideal audience wants you to solve for them.

Schedule Your Shows

As an avid podcast listener, I've been trained by my favorite shows to anticipate *when* new episodes are coming out.

For example, my favorite Christian-themed show, *John Eldredge and Ransomed Heart,* comes out every single Monday morning without fail.

In fact, I wake up every Monday, open the Podcast App on my iPhone and immediately download the most recent episode. I then hook up Rosie the Dog to a leash, pop in my earphones and walk the trail behind our home, diving in with a group of people I've spent the past five years listening to religiously (no pun intended).

The Ransomed Heart Podcast has *trained me* as a listener for when I should expect each new episode. You want to do the same thing by publishing your episodes on a consistent and predictable schedule.

The "when" doesn't matter (meaning what day of the week or time of day) nearly as much as just doing it on the *same* day/time each week. Remember, most people consume your podcast "on demand," meaning when it's convenient for them to listen. They just need to know *when* to anticipate new episodes coming out.

What To Measure

Podcasts have plenty of metrics, and advertisers or big-name guests will want to know how many listens or downloads each episode gets as a measure of how popular your podcast truly is. But beyond using these stats to lure advertisers or big-name guests, don't sweat the numbers.

As I'll continue to say until I'm out of breath, you cannot deposit likes, comments or listens into your bank account!

Focus instead on the *engagement* your podcast produces. Are you seeing people emailing you or hitting a landing page you set up with a free lead magnet when you mention those as a Call To Action (CTA) in a specific episode?

Are the *quality* of leads coming in from your podcast significantly higher and easier to turn into paying customers than the leads you get from Facebook Ads as another example?

Remember, if someone ends up liking your podcast, they will *really* like it. They will go through and binge-listen to multiple episodes in a single day. They will get to know, like and trust you as if they were sitting down for hours at a time listening to you pontificate inside a coffee shop.

So, while the *volume* of leads you generate with a podcast might not be as large as other content marketing methods, the *quality* of those leads is going to be sky high.

How To Promote and Grow Your Podcast

It's important to realize that just because you publish a podcast doesn't mean everyone will immediately listen.

While it's true that Podcast distribution networks like Apple's iTunes platform function as large search engines, helping your podcast get "discovered" when someone types in a search term or phrase related to the topic of your show, you need to actively share and promote your podcast to grow your audience.

As of this writing, one of the big factors in growing your podcast on platforms like iTunes is user reviews and ratings, so *always* be asking for those!

Just like with asking for a review of your book on Amazon, you'll want to ask *anyone* who emails you or mentions your podcast online for a rating and review.

Here's a simple script you can use:

"Thanks so much for your note about the podcast! What have you found most helpful or thought-provoking so far? Also, if you have a moment, could you leave me a review on iTunes? Reviews help a TON as far as helping others discover the show, so I'm beyond grateful if you have a moment to leave me a quick review. Here's a link if you're up for it - [insert URL]. Thanks again!"

The script above encourages more engagement by asking the listener a specific question about what he or she has found helpful from the podcast, and then pivots to request a small favor (the review).

Remember: If you don't ask, most people aren't going to go out of their way to leave your podcast a review or rating. So ask!

Guest of Honor

Another great way to quickly grow your podcast is to be a guest on someone else's podcast.

Given the way the medium works, it makes sense that if a listener of someone else's podcast loved an interview you did, he or she would also likely enjoy *your* podcast.

When it comes to asking someone else if you can be a guest on his or her podcast, you need to *earn* the right to ask the host for time in front of his or her audience.

For example, I earned my way onto an episode of *Entrepreneur On Fire* by contacting John Lee Dumas "cold" via email and offering to rewrite his entire LinkedIn profile for free - no strings attached.

I didn't put into my initial emails with John and his team that I was angling for an guest interview on his insanely popular podcast. Rather, I just introduced myself, explained I was a fan of John and the show, and wanted to bring him some value and help around LinkedIn. I also made it clear that I would do 100 percent of the work, without requiring a single second of John's time or attention. And, once I was done, I'd submit a draft of what I'd come up with to John and his team, and if he liked it, he could copy-and-paste the text I'd created into his LinkedIn profile. And, if he didn't like it, no worries - I was just happy for the chance to try and help him out.

Long story short, I worked my tail off, JLD loved what I did, and by *demonstrating* my authority instead of just claiming it, he was open to my request later on to appear on his show to talk about LinkedIn marketing.

I'd also built in a natural "hook" into my episode of *Entrepreneur on Fire,* with John being able to tell the *story* of how this guy John Nemo approached him out of the blue, knocked his socks off by redoing JLD's LinkedIn profile in a great way, and the quick wins and results JLD witnessed as a result.

This cannot be overlooked, especially with Podcasts - people need a *narrative* to attach to you. They need a *story to tell* about why you do what you do, how you got here, etc. You can't simply show up with information and expertise and expect to dazzle an audience.

The Echo of Your "Big" Interviews

One big benefit of being a guest on well-known podcasts like *Entrepreneur On Fire* is that many other smaller shows will reach out to and ask you to be a guest on *their shows* as well.

I've found this true time and again. I do the upfront work to earn the chance (and it's only a chance, nothing is guaranteed!) to be on a big-name show. And, if I succeed, meaning I get on the show as a guest and do a great job, dozens of other smaller podcasts in the same niche contact me asking for an interview.

It becomes seamless and easy to book those additional guest appearances, because they've already heard me on the "big" show and know I'll be a good guest and share valuable information with the audience.

Short Runs vs. Deep Passes

If you think of an American football analogy, being a guest on smaller podcasts is like getting a 3 yard gain running the ball up the middle. If you do it enough times, you move the ball down the field, and while you don't get an immediate or massive payoff, you keep moving forward toward your goal.

Now, once in a while, you might try (and hit on) a big pass play by landing on a major show. With these attempts, there's much more risk (doing the work to *earn* that opportunity, because it's not guaranteed someone will feature you on his or her show at the end of your efforts) and reward involved, just like with throwing a deep bomb of a pass into triple coverage along the sideline.

Pitching Yourself

When you ask to be on someone's Podcast (large or small), there are certain ways to increase your chances of getting booked. For instance, you'll want to approach shows that fit your brand or expertise.

If you've got social proof (big name clients you've worked with or gotten testimonials from, books you've published, etc.) those are important markers for a Podcast host to know you're legit.

You'll also need some samples of your interviews, whether it's a link to your own podcast or you on someone else's show. You want those sample episodes to showcase your communication style, insight and wisdom on a specific topic.

Also, once you appear on a few shows, you can leverage those credits to pitch yourself to more shows. For instance, if someone sees you've also been featured on other shows in their genre, and if you have links to those episodes or appearances to prove it, that makes you a safer booking for the podcast host.

I think back to when I worked in talk radio as a producer and on-air talent. I was *always* looking for great guests, and loved when, instead of me chasing someone, *they chased me* and did my work for me.

Do The Work For Them!

For example, write up a sample list of questions the podcast host can ask you about the specific topic you want to speak on. Make the questions curiosity-invoking, the type that the host would be *dying* to discover the answers too.

For example, when I offer to be a guest on someone's podcast to talk about using LinkedIn for lead generation, I'd start with sample questions they can ask me like these:

"So you have a pretty crazy story. Back in 2012, you quit a safe, six figure day job and decided to build a business from scratch using only LinkedIn. Why did you do that, and what happened as a result?"

(The answer to this goes into my origin story about how I was able to generate $135,000 USD of revenue in just 90 days from new clients I found on LinkedIn, and how I realized early on LinkedIn could be used like a giant search engine for B2B prospects.)

"You say 99 percent of people are using LinkedIn the wrong way. What do you mean by that?"

Or, if I know the podcast audience will appreciate and remember one of my favorite lyrical poets from the 1990s, I'll phrase the sample question this way:

"Not sure about this one - You say Vanilla Ice holds the key to creating a lead-generating LinkedIn profile. I think you're going to need to explain this one a bit further, John!"

(With either version of the question, the answer dives into making your LinkedIn profile what I call client-facing instead of having it read like a résumé. I quote the Vanilla Ice lyric, *"If you got a problem, yo' I'll solve it"* as an example of having a profile that talks about the key problems you solve for your ideal clients.)

See how much better those types of questions are instead of, *"Tell us about how you first decided to use LinkedIn for lead generation."* or *"Do you have any tips on improving one's LinkedIn profile?"*

Load up those suggested interview questions with drama and curiosity, and your host is going to get excited for the chance to speak with you. Remember, you want these questions to set the stage for *stories* that illustrate the concepts you want to teach.

It's called *info-tainment,* my friends.

Get some!

This is Critical

Also, harkening back to my days doing PR, the more you can do someone's job for him, the more likely he or she is to allow you to be a part of his or her podcast.

Send those suggested interview questions. Explain how, given the research you've done on this person's show, you feel like your topic dovetails perfectly with other episodes he or she has done on Topic XYZ. (And name those specific episodes so the host knows you really have checked out the podcast.)

Talk about the show's format, and how you feel like your explanation of Topic XYZ will fit perfectly as part of the show's section on XYZ.

Ask. Feature. Promote.

Another great avenue to grow your Podcast quickly is to leverage the online platforms of the guests you interview.

For example, if you feature someone on your podcast to talk about a topic and promote his or her new book, he or she is naturally going to return the favor by sending traffic to the show so his or her fans can hear the interview.

Make sure you (again) make the other person's job easy, sending him or her pre-written social media status updates with a link to the episode, or even writing an email he or she can send to his or her list with info about the episode, what made it unique, why they'll want to listen, etc.

Make it copy-and-paste simple for your guests to promote their appearances on your show, and they'll send traffic your way!

How To Get Guests on Your Podcast

If you want to do an interview-based show, in the beginning, at least, it will be difficult to score big-name guests assuming your podcast is brand new. However, you can entice people to come on by promising to promote the episode via your social media channels, email list, even taking out paid Facebook Ads if you want to go that far.

If you make it clear to the potential guest who your ideal audience is and how you will promote the other person to that audience in meaningful ways, he or she will find it harder to say "no" as long as your audience is one they want to reach.

Also, once you land that first big-name guest, it's *far* easier to get others to come on your show. Here's an example of how to leverage that approach:

"Hey [NAME], I'd love to have you on my podcast to talk about [Topic XYZ]. We've also had [Big Name they will recognize from their niche or industry] on and it went great, and I think our audience will love what you have to share as well!"

Bottom line: If you want to land big interviews, do what you have to do (even offering to take out paid advertising!) in order to make it worth your guests' while to come on the show.

Remember, John Lee Dumas toiled and hustled for *years* chasing and booking guests 7 days a week for *Entrepreneur on Fire* long before the likes of Tony Robbins *asked* to come on.

Podcast growth doesn't happen overnight, and it can be slow, building 1 listener at a time.

It's worth it, however, because the *quality* of sales leads you get from your podcasting audience is as good as it gets for business.

Confidence is Key

Another thing about podcasts: Sitting in front of a microphone and talking to strangers can be terrifying.

You have to get over yourself and your internal critics *("I hate the sound of my voice, nobody will want to hear what I have to say, etc.")* fast if you want to be successful in creating a podcast people listen to.

Confidence and enthusiasm in your voice and delivery are contagious. So too are fear and doubt. If you sound nervous, uncertain or passive, your audience will pick up on it and tune out.

If it helps, visualize yourself talking to your biggest fan, that one client or customer who can't get enough of what you have to say. Someone who hangs on your every word, who *loves* the way you explain things and the communication style you employ.

Remember, when you sit down to record a podcast, *that one person is who you are talking to,* not the "masses" or strangers or critics.

Podcasts, by nature, are intimate conversations and discussions that happen inside someone's head (thanks to earphones) in a 1-to-1 fashion.

Also, note the word *conversation.*

Don't script and "read" your podcast into a microphone. You'll sound like an actor over-rehearsing for a play and be stilted and boring in your delivery.

Instead, *talk!*

Be colloquial in your communication style. Laugh, joke and roll with where you're going on a topic.

Instead of preparing a detailed script, just jot down a few key topics or points you want to make sure you cover, and the order to address them in, and then riff about those points conversationally.

Great Stories = Podcast Gold

If you can, start with a fun story on how you came across a certain concept or topic, or share a personal experience that really drove home the point or lesson to you.

Here's a perfect example: A few months ago I listened to a podcast where a guy named Tim Paige was giving tons of great advice about how to create a high-converting webinar that sells your products or services.

Because it's been several weeks, I don't remember much of the interview, but what I *do* remember was delivered via a story Tim told about his days doing door-to-door vacuum cleaner sales.

Tim sold an ultra expensive, high-end vacuum cleaner that was like $3,000, and he had to do it door-to-door with strangers who'd never met him before.

Instead of trying to talk his way inside to demonstrate all the values and benefits of the vacuum and *then* reveal the price at the very end of his presentation, Tim flipped the script.

Right away, he'd tell the person at the door, "So, this vacuum costs $3,000, and I'm sure you're not thinking you'd ever want to spend that much on a vacuum. But if you'd at least like to see what a $3,000 vacuum can do, I can bring it inside and show you a few things."

By getting the elephant in the room (the high price) out of the way immediately, Tim was able to break that fear or focus his audience had on the price *("Yeah, yeah, this is a cool product and presentation, but what's it going to cost me!")* so they could focus on the actual *content* of his presentation.

With the price question/fear out of the way, many consumers ended up inviting Tim into their home, curious to see just what a $3,000 vacuum really *could* do. By using this unexpected approach, Tim got into more homes, did his vacuum demo and ended up selling scores of units as a result.

He decided to apply the same strategy to webinars, telling people early on, "Look, I *do* have a great online course called [XYZ], and it costs [dollar amount], but I don't want you to get hung up and worried about that right now. Instead, let's just focus on the free content, tips and training I promised to share with you today. And, if you're wanting to go deeper and learn more at the end of our time together, we can talk about how to get [Online Course Name] and some special bonuses that come with it. Sound good? Great! Let's dive in."

Even though it's been several months since I heard Tim's podcast interview, that one particular *story* about his door-to-door vacuum sales days helped embed a webinar sales strategy I'll never forget.

You want to do something similar with *your* podcast content - tell a great story that helps people *encode and remember* the lesson or strategy you want them to walk away with.

Headlines Are Key

Just like with blogs and other pieces of content, Podcast headlines matter far more than you realize. Needless to say, you *must* come up with curiosity-invoking Podcast episode titles.

Not just *"Interview with [Name] on [Topic]"* or *"Episode 48: [Topic]."*

Instead, make it dramatic and invoke some curiosity!

For example, I decided to create a Podcast episode out of a sales strategy I found in a book that I bought for $1.99 online.

So, instead of titling the Podcast *"[Name of Sales Strategy based on Book Title]"* I went with with this headline instead:

"The $2 Book Worth (at Least) $20k in Extra Sales."

I then furthered the story by making this the first line of the Podcast episode description:

"I found it for $1.99 online, and what I read in the first chapter alone will make it worth 10,000 times that in value. I share the name of the book, the $20k lesson I learned and the one daily habit you must develop in order to be successful in this episode of the Nemo Radio Podcast!"

See what I'm doing here? With both the Podcast title and opening lines of the episode description, I'm hooking you into a story and playing on your curiosity to get you to listen.

(Note: To get a look at the latest podcasting tools, software and strategies I use to create episodes of Nemo Radio, go to https://ContentMarketingMachine.com/Bonus)

Chapter 10:
The Single Best Content Marketing Tool I've Ever Seen

What you hold in your hand at this very moment is the single best content marketing and lead generating tool I've ever utilized in nearly a decade of doing business on my own.

In my experience, books (yes, books!) are the single *best* form of content marketing on the planet. Best of all, it's never been easier to write, publish and sell your book online immediately via Amazon.com and other retailers.

As I alluded to earlier in *this* book, the gatekeepers are long gone across all types of media - including publishing and selling books to a global audience.

You don't need a literary agent. You don't need a publisher. You don't need permission or approval. You get to write, edit and publish your book *for free* on Amazon, and the *marketplace* gets to decide if it's worth reading.

(And, given the fact that pretty much every book sold on the planet right now seems to come from Amazon, you can trust that the marketplace there is going to be a great indicator!)

Before I dive into all the semantics and strategies behind publishing a book as part of your content marketing strategy, let's take a look at *why* books are such a valuable tool.

Books Build Authority

Simply put, if you've written a book, you have a leg up on the competition.

In fact, people can say, "Meet [NAME] - she *literally* wrote the book on [TOPIC]" when introducing you for presentations, interviews or to colleagues.

Even with the ease of self-publishing in today's marketplace allowing *anyone* to write and publish a book in short order, there's still a special aura or sense of authority that you carry in the minds of your ideal audience as the author of a book.

In fact, it's like the pre-Internet days of having your own TV program or talk radio show - being an *Author* (capital "A") means something in the credibility department. It's an instant trust factor that moves you up a notch in the mind of a prospect.

Especially if you do any sort of professional speaking, consulting or coaching, a book serves as sort of a golden ticket to catch the time, interest and attention of people in your target audience.

Books are Business Cards on Steroids

There's no better way to introduce (and indoctrinate!) someone to your style of communication and the systems and strategies related to your business than handing him or her a copy of your book.

Best of all, you don't have to spend any time or effort explaining yourself to a prospective client or customer. Instead, your book does all the heavy lifting, helping people get to know, like and trust you *before* they even talk to you face-to-face!

Think about your own experience with the books you love. Aren't you a bit in awe of the author once you finish? Wouldn't you be thrilled to have a chance to talk with him or her directly, even for just a few moments?

Of course you would - and so too will the people who read (and love) *your* book.

A well-written book gives people all the ingredients they need to decide if you're worth doing business with, helping pre-sell and pre-qualify your best prospects ahead of time so you don't have to.

If someone comes into your email list and sales funnel through one of your books, they are *infinitely* more qualified and ready-to-buy when compared to someone who came in via a Facebook Ad or other online lead generation methods.

Books Are (Perceived as) High Value Content

Speaking of building your email list … Of all the different lead magnets I've offered over the years, far and away the most successful one has been giving away a free copy of my book, *LinkedIn Riches.*

To clarify, I'm *not* talking about a short "eBook" that is little more than a glorified PDF someone put together. Rather, I'm talking about a *book,* a full length, nonfiction business book.

Here's what the landing page looks like on the front of my LinkedIn Riches website:

(Note: I'm not mailing people a print copy of the book in this circumstance. Instead, I offer them a free Kindle or iBooks version to read digitally, or else the audiobook version as a .mp3 file.)

Giving away your *entire* book as a lead magnet is super attractive because almost nobody does that. Many authors might offer a few free chapters, or the "Free + Shipping" upsell offer online marketers like Russell Brunson have made famous, but nobody just straight up *gives* you his or her entire book for free online.

One common reason for this is many authors believe you'll cannibalize (or even eliminate entirely!) your book sales if people know they can get a copy for free on your website.

In my experience, however, this simply isn't true. In fact, I've sold the same amount of *LinkedIn Riches* books on Amazon every single month for several years now despite giving away the book for free on the front page of my website.

Here's why: The Internet is a big place. Shockingly, not everybody has *heard* of John Nemo or his book about LinkedIn. (I know, it's hard for me to believe too.)

Instead, many (and I mean many!) people go to Amazon.com and utilize it like a Search Engine, typing in a topic (i.e. *LinkedIn*) they're interested in reading more about.

When they do, Amazon works like Google, surfacing a slew of books that cover all things LinkedIn.

As a result, people who have never heard of me or my website end up "finding" my book on Amazon and buying it.

Over the years, I've sold so many copies of *LinkedIn Riches* that Amazon now surfaces my book title as one of its suggested search terms when you type "LinkedIn" into Amazon's search bar:

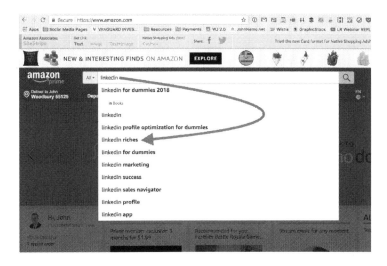

How cool is that?

Now, I don't share this to brag, but rather to illustrate *what is possible* when you format and frame your book the right way on Amazon.

Before I better understood the online animal that is Amazon, I self-published several other books beginning in the early 2000s. To this day, none them sell as well as *LinkedIn Riches* does.

The reason is simple - I didn't understand *how* to market my books (both fiction and nonfiction) on Amazon, such as including the right keywords, phrases and search terms on my book description page, along with generating lots of reader reviews and ratings, which help the book surface more on Amazon searches, and so on.

(More on how to do all this later - there are a lot of moving parts on how to get your book selling well on Amazon.)

Long story short, publishing your book on Amazon will *not* crater your overall book sales, because so many people who go to Amazon every day *have never heard of you or your website,* so they're not looking there for your book to begin with.

With *LinkedIn Riches,* I get the best of both worlds - steady sales every single day from new people who "find" me on Amazon, and email subscribers from people I send to my website via various free traffic generation methods (Podcast interviews where I mention a link to the free book, guest blogs I write with a link to my website, 1-on-1 LinkedIn messages I send to new connections, etc.)

Even if giving away my book for free online *did* impact my sales in a negative way, I'd still do it.

Here's why: I make around $3 USD to $5 USD per copy of *LinkedIn Riches* that sells on Amazon. (It depends if it's print, digital or audiobook, what country the person is in, etc.)

I make anywhere from $1497 USD to $1997 USD for every unit of my *LinkedIn Riches* Online Course that I sell. And the #1 source of new customers for the online course comes via people who *first* read the book, then sign up for my sales webinar and purchase the online course.

(In my content marketing approach, I position my LinkedIn Riches book as the appetizer, whereas the online course is the steak dinner and dessert. The book gives you a great overview of what is possible when it comes to utilizing LinkedIn to generate leads, along with some specific strategies and approaches. Taking off from there, the online course is all that strategy in action, showing you specifically how to find and engage your ideal clients on LinkedIn, including training videos, copy-and-paste scripts and more.)

Now, if you think about the product or service you sell, and what you *already* spend on digital or print advertising, wouldn't you be happy paying $3 USD to $5 USD per qualified lead?

Even if everyone who gets a free copy of my *LinkedIn Riches* book "costs" me $3 USD to $5 USD (assuming I could convince them to buy the book instead over on Amazon, which is no sure thing), it's still a great ROI for me considering my end result is selling a $1997 USD online course to a certain percentage of those readers.

Not to mention all the people who *don't* buy the full course, but who, thanks to going through my book, join my email list (I insert different URLs inside the book where you can get free training videos and resources related to the book's content). Once those people are on my email list, they are exposed to additional products, services and special offers I have available. Or those who don't buy the course but who love the book might end up referring a friend or colleague to me for 1-on-1 coaching, the online course or something else.

Bottom line: The best marketing decision I ever made was giving away my book *LinkedIn Riches* for free. It's grown my email list like a weed, pre-qualified and pre-sold top prospects on purchasing my $1997 USD online course and allowed me to build real, meaningful authority and engagement with thousands of people *without* having to talk to them all personally one at a time.

Playing the Long Game

In addition, books aren't "here and gone" like a blog post or video, washed away a day later in the digital stream of content that flows nonstop through our devices and computers.

For instance, I first published *LinkedIn Riches* in 2014 and then re-released it with updated content in 2016. Today, all these years later, it *still* does all the heavy lifting for me day after day with my content marketing and lead generation. In addition, the momentum the book gained (and then sustained) on Amazon has kept sales steady there too, with more people "finding" and purchasing it every day.

Depending on your topic, you'll want to make sure you keep the content of your book evergreen, meaning you don't have to go back and update it every few months. As an example, the first edition of *LinkedIn Riches* (published in 2014) talked a lot about specific features and tools you could utilize on the platform at the time. Of course, being a digital platform, LinkedIn changes all the time, adding and removing various features and tools. I realized, when penning an updated version in 2016, that I was better off emphasizing the evergreen strategies and approaches of how to find, engage and sell on LinkedIn instead of talking in-depth about the various tools and digital elements of the platform.

As a result, the book stays relevant, because the strategies and concepts I teach don't change like online tools do. And, even better, it gives me an excuse to get people out of the book and onto my email list, as I invite them to a landing page online to get my most updated free training videos, tools and resources based on the strategies in the book.

Books = Appetizers

When it comes to the content marketing strategy behind your book, you want to think of it like a dinner party.

Your book should be the tasty appetizer, whetting your audience's appetite for the main course - your paid product or service. And, like a good appetizer, your book is going to warm up and increase the appetite your audience has for you, your style of communication, your systems and strategies, and so on.

To continue the food analogy, your book can be like sharing your favorite recipe, while your paid product or service is like you coming over, bringing all the ingredients and doing all the cooking yourself for the audience.

After all, the more access, expertise and insight someone wants from you or your company, the more he or she should expect to pay.

Take It Online

One of the best lead generation strategies you can utilize with a book is inviting readers to go online and get access to additional free materials (training videos, a list of suggested tools or resources, scripts, etc.) that build off the content from the book.

With digital eBooks, it's easy to include a clickable hyperlink that takes someone from his or her device right to a landing page on your website.

With print or audiobooks, you'll want to create and mention a short, easy-to-type URL that leads to your landing page online.

Either way, you *always* want to embrace the opportunity to build your email list and move people further into your sales funnel by offering additional (and free) content, tools, tips and trainings based on the book.

(For example, by now you've noticed I've included multiple links to various resources, interviews or other online content related to what you're reading in this book right now.)

That doesn't mean you have to "hold back" or *not* share your best tips, techniques and strategies in a book.

Far from it!

In fact, if you *don't* share your best content and help others get quick wins and value as a result, you won't win enough trust to ensure your audience even *wants* more of your content online or anywhere else.

Making it Happen

As I mentioned earlier, self-publishing has completely changed the game when it comes to writing and publishing books in order to reach a massive, global audience.

And, as I'll explain in just a bit, you don't have to write an enormous tome or The Next Great American Novel to get in on the action.

Here's why: Short books that introduce an idea or strategy that delivers a quick win or solves a problem for your ideal audience are a great way to introduce your business or brand to Amazon users and other online audiences.

And, if you follow the strategy I outlined earlier, making a short, self-published book (think, "appetizer") available via Amazon for little to no cost (yes, you can give away Kindle versions of your book for free!) is a great way to leverage content marketing to build your email list and move readers deeper into your sales funnel.

The semantics are actually quite simple.

You can write, edit and format your book for free online using a platform like Google Docs.

Next, you can export and save your book as an .epub file right from Google Docs, meaning it's ready for anyone to read using Kindle, Apple iBooks or similar e-reader platforms.

Finally, you can utilize a platform like Amazon CreateSpace (www.CreateSpace. com) to upload your finished book and make it available for sale on Amazon. com. CreateSpace even has free book cover templates you can utilize to create your own book cover if you need to!

See how easy and cost efficient this is?

There's no excuse for you not to take advantage, and the daunting idea of having to write an entire book from scratch is also a fallacy.

Instead, you can repurpose existing blog posts or other written content you have and turn them into a short book that you can sell or (better yet) give away on Amazon as a way to generate leads with your content.

Quality Matters

While you *can* do this entire process for free, I would recommend spending money to have someone design an eye-catching, attractive front cover for your book. (And a back cover if you plan on also making your book available via a print version as well.)

The reason being, people *do* judge a book by its cover, even online, and a sloppy, amateur-ish looking cover will kill any chance of someone getting past that to read your content (however good it might be!) on the inside.

So, if you need to, spend the money on finding a great designer to come up with an awesome book cover. There are lots (and I mean lots!) of freelance designers and freelance gig websites out there to utilize.

(For a recommendation on book cover resources, including who I recommend, visit https://ContentMarketingMachine.com/Bonus)

Like anything else, the actual *content* of your book should follow the same strategies and principles I've already covered so far in these pages.

Once you have your book written, edited and polished, along with a great cover, you can upload it for free to Amazon via CreateSpace and then separately (if you like) via iTunes to Apple's iBooks online store.

Audiobooks = Big Impact

Similar to podcasts, audiobooks have also enjoyed massive growth in recent years thanks to the advent of "on the go" listening via smart phones and other devices.

Just like with print and digital books on Amazon, you can record your own audiobook and then upload it for free using Amazon's ACX platform. (www.acx.com). Or, you can hire (through ACX's freelance marketplace or other freelance sites) a narrator to turn your print or digital book into an eBook by recording the audio for you.

Either way, once you have the audio files on hand, you can upload them for free through ACX and begin selling your audiobook via Amazon, Audible.com and iTunes, which are three of the top audiobook retailers in the world.

Advice on Audiobooks

While it can be a lot of work to record and narrate your own audiobook, I cannot emphasize enough the power and *quality* of the leads you will generate as a result.

Similar to podcasts, with an audiobook, your voice (if you do your own narration) is literally in your audience's head for hours on end.

Next to face-to-face meetings or online video, *nothing* fills up those know, like and trust buckets with a prospect faster than hearing your voice in his or her head.

So, if you decide to create an audiobook (even a short one), I cannot suggest strongly enough that you do the narration yourself. After all, if *you* are the brand as a Business Coach or Consultant, or as the point of contact for your company, you want people to get to know, like and trust you by hearing *your* voice.

Also, it can be tedious recording an audiobook, depending on how long it is and how many "takes" you need in order to record each chapter. Having narrated several audiobooks of my own, I found that it's far easier (and better received by readers) if I just talk or riff about the key concepts in a chapter, telling stories and being conversational instead of trying to read verbatim what I wrote for the print or digital version of the book.

Trying to read your own written book into a microphone can (at least to me!) come across as stilted and rehearsed, whereas telling stories and being conversational (without worrying about following a script) is easier to record and more enjoyable for the listener.

Better yet, not having the pressure of focusing on a script so you don't miss a word means you're more relaxed and at ease emotionally, allowing you to insert more energy, passion and emotion into your performance.

Think of recording your audiobook (and your podcast) as a conversation between you and your ideal client or customer. You're conversational, friendly, have energy and enthusiasm in your tone of voice, and you tell great stories that make the other person laugh, cry or *feel* something important as you drive home the lessons and concepts.

Now that we have some of the semantics out of the way, how do we go about ensuring people find and engage with your books on Amazon and other online platforms?

The British (Book Marketing) Invasion

As a proud American, it's embarrassing to concede, given the whole Revolutionary War, Mr. Bean and everything else, but I have to admit - sometimes you can learn a thing or two from the British.

Case in point: As I mentioned earlier, I've authored 8 books and have been self-publishing since the early 2000s. And I was missing something massive.

A guy named Nick Stephenson (a Brit) showed me what it was.

The Big Realization

Here's what Nick taught me: if you want to grow your audience with your content (books in particular), you must be on Amazon.com, and (most important) you must think of Amazon not as an online retailer, but as a huge Search Engine.

If Content is King, Amazon is The Queen

In today's marketplace, content is currency.

The better quality content you create and share online, the better quality audience you attract, and the easier it becomes to sell your products and services as a result.

What impressed me with Nick Stephenson's unique approach to Amazon was how you can repurpose the free content you already have (blog posts, eBooks, white papers, etc.) as free or low-cost eBooks on Amazon.

Given how targeted and deep Amazon goes with its niches, audience intelligence and search functionality, the site makes it easy for you to get "discovered" by a whole new audience - Amazon's more than 300 million active users.

Ready to Buy

Remember, when someone jumps on Amazon, he or she is ready to purchase something that will solve a problem he or she has. So, once an Amazon user "finds" your content sitting on the site as an attractive, low-cost (or even free) solution to his or her challenge, it becomes a no-brainer to give it a look.

And once someone starts consuming your content, whole new worlds open up for both you and the reader!

Proof Positive

As I shared earlier, Nick's approach worked so well for me on Amazon that *LinkedIn Riches* is now a suggested search term when you type in the word "LinkedIn" on the platform.

There's no reason you can't do the same thing.

Who is This Guy?

Back to the whole British thing.

I first stumbled across Nick Stephenson on (you guessed it) Amazon.

He's a bestselling author and online trainer who helps entrepreneurs, business owners and authors grow and build audiences online by leveraging Amazon.

I won't go on singing his praises, because yes, I'm a proud American, and we like thinking we're the ones that come up with these types of great insights and ideas.

But, long story short, I went through all of Nick's content (from his free digital books that first caught my eye on Amazon to his paid online course) and got immense value from it.

The key concepts of Nick's program are fairly simple - you figure out what the ideal Amazon keywords, search terms and phrases are related to your specific book, and then you format specific sections of your book's description page, categories and other areas in order to ensure it gets "found" properly on Amazon.

In addition, you can utilize several different strategies (contests, free giveaways, Facebook Ads, etc.) to drive traffic to your book's Amazon page, and, the more people who download or purchase it, the more Amazon realizes it's something people want, and surfaces it higher and higher on results pages. In addition, using some specific strategies and scripts with happy readers you engage with generates enough book reviews and ratings to help the book stay high up in search results and even get added to category-specific bestseller lists.

Nick breaks it all down in his free and paid content, and if you want to see how it works, start with his free eBook, "Reader Magnets."

Here's a link to the eBook: https://uf254.isrefer.com/go/ebook/johnnemo/

(Note: This is my affiliate link, so if you end up enjoying Nick's free eBook and eventually decide to purchase his paid course like I did, I get an affiliate commission. However, you don't pay anything extra.)

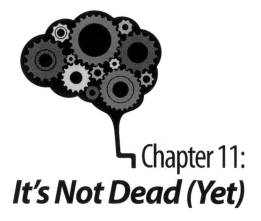

Chapter 11:
It's Not Dead (Yet)

B logs have been around as long as the Internet has existed, and, in recent decades "bloggers" have gone from someone living in his or her mom's basement to full-scale, credentialed professional entities covering professional sports teams, businesses and other entities.

In addition, the most popular bloggers wield enormous influence, monetizing their platforms via display ads, sponsored posts or other methods.

That isn't the avenue I want to explore right now, other than to say this: *Blogs still matter.* As much as everyone (myself included) hypes video, audio, virtual reality or whatever else comes along in terms of content creation, people still consume blogs online.

Especially if your audience skews into an older demographic (meaning those who grew up reading newspapers and books, or even the early days of the Internet when blogs were about all you really saw online) blogging should be a critical part of your content marketing strategy.

Frequency vs. Quality

Today, the ubiquitous nature of blogging means *everyone* has a blog, and that you publishing or sharing a blog post isn't anything new, special or exciting ... unless the *quality* is such that your content cannot be ignored.

Hear me well, dear reader: Do *not* embrace the strategy of trying to churn out as much copy (i.e. blogs) as you can each week, publishing anything that comes to mind or fills "space" online.

Instead, embrace *quality over quantity.* Make your blogs invaluable for your audience. Solve real problems. Deliver quick wins. Tell great stories.

And then, promote and share the heck out of it! Make sure people know about your blog posts, see them and get a chance to consume them. You're better off only having a few pieces of truly great content and reminding online audiences about them repeatedly versus cranking out tons of mediocre blogs in the name of having something "new" to share each day or week of your online existence.

How To Grow Your Audience With Guest Blogging

Blogging is a great way to cultivate and grow an online following, especially if you post *guest blogs* on someone else's website. Guest blogging is a fantastic way to leverage someone else's platform and existing audience in order to promote your content, similar to having a guest column published in a newspaper or magazine.

Especially if you do a good job in your actual guest blog of including links back to your website (when appropriate) and a CTA (Call To Action) for the audience to obtain more info as it relates to the topic of your post, you will generate lots of traffic back to your website and opt-ins to grow your email list. (It also helps your SEO rankings, which is never a bad thing!)

Even better, you grow your credibility, add social proof and increase authority in the eyes of others online by having a list of websites and/or publications that have published your content online.

How To Pitch Your Guest Blogging Services

To get going with guest blogging, start by identifying the ideal online publications and/or websites where your ideal audience *already* consumes content. Then approach the editors of those sites and pitch your availability to submit guest blogs that would appeal to their audience.

It's important to note that many larger websites and publications have very specific guidelines or processes on how to apply for guest blogging positions. Other, smaller sites might be easier to break in with, because here's the bottom line: *everyone* needs fresh content to share with their audience as often as possible.

As much as possible, frame your "pitch" to these sites around how and why your content will provide great value and engagement to *their* existing audience. For instance, if it's an industry news site you're approaching, and pitching the idea of adding you as a weekly contributor with a blog on a related area or strategic approach that goes beyond what the site typically has featured.

Who To Approach for Guest Blogs

In particular, someone who serves your ideal audience but who is *not* a direct competitor makes ideal sense for you to approach with the offer to provide guest blogs.

For instance, there are lots of "news" type online publications and websites for various industries where your content will be a perfect compliment to the day's news, case studies, trends, etc.

There might also be someone who provides a complimentary product or service to the same audience you serve, and perhaps they'd love some fresh content (via your guest blogs) to share on their site each week as a value-add for their existing customers and prospects.

The "Cost" of Guest Blogging

Bottom Line: Think about where your audience goes to consume industry-specific content, and then pitch *those* sites on adding your expertise and content (at no cost to the website) to the various offerings it puts out each day.

That's right, do your guest blogging for free. Sure, it's nice if people want to pay you to write and publish your original content on their website, but it's very rare. Also, it's much more valuable to get the exposure, social proof and quality traffic guest blogging provides than making a few bucks for publishing a post on someone else's platform.

Keep in mind, too, that you can *repurpose* those guest blogs you write and use that content elsewhere, including on your own website and other platforms.

Depending on what site you post your guest blog to, they may require "exclusive" publishing rights for a period of time *before* you can post your piece of content anywhere else online.

For example, when I wrote guest blogs for *Inc. Magazine, American City Business Journals* and other online publications, they required "first" and "exclusive" access to my posts for a set period of time before I could re-publish or repurpose those same pieces on my website or anywhere else.

Once that period was up, however, I could take the same posts, tweak the headline and a few other sections if needed, and re-publish them online on my blog or other sites.

Leveraging LinkedIn to Promote Your Blog Posts

One of my favorite (and most effective) ways to promote blog posts to a target audience is using 1-on-1 LinkedIn messages.

While I won't go into my entire LinkedIn strategy here (you can get all kinds of free trainings and a free copy of my book "LinkedIn Riches" at www.LinkedInRiches.com) I will break down how I use 1-on-1 LinkedIn messages *after* I've already connected to my ideal reader for a specific blog post.

The key is *not* just spamming people with a link to your post, assuming they want to read it.

Instead, the people you meet on LinkedIn (or any other social platform) want you to *ask permission* before you start trying to sell them.

This 1-on-1 messaging script does that, and, in addition to working like crazy, it also doesn't make people angry, offended or upset when they receive it from me.

It's a two part script, and you can start utilizing this approach when you message prospects on LinkedIn or other social media platforms to promote your blog posts.

Here's part 1 of the script, and notice how it is conversational and friendly in its tone:

Hey [NAME] – hope you are well!

Curious – Are you interested in [TOPIC]?

(Note: "Topic" is the topic of your blog, and should be phrased as a *benefit* the reader would want. As an example, you would write: "Curious - are you interested in using LinkedIn to find new clients?" as your sentence. The blog post you deliver is going to be about how to use LinkedIn to get clients, obviously, and you're framing it up as such!)

If so, I have a great blog post that explains how you can [Get Benefit XYZ].

(Note: *"Get Benefit XYZ"* relates to the previous sentence, and reinforces to the reader the topic of your blog and why he or she would want to read your post.)

If you'd like to see how it works, just reply with the word "YES" and I can shoot you over a link to the post.

(Note: I give them a simple CTA ["reply with the word YES"] since people are busy, might be accessing my message on a mobile device and just need a simple command to follow if they are indeed interested in reading the blog.)

And if you're not interested, no worries at all.

Cheers!

Now, if the person replies to my 1-on-1 LinkedIn message with a "YES" or thumbs up emoji or something similar to indicate he or she is open to reading the post, I copy-and-paste the following response back to each individual:

Awesome!

Here's a link to the post: [URL]

Can't wait to hear your thoughts!

(Note: I typically make the URL link *away* from LinkedIn and instead take the reader over to my personal blog or website, because I want that person spending time on *my* digital turf [my website and blog] where he or she can quickly and easily learn more about me and my services instead of keeping the conversation over on LinkedIn.)

Notice, there are four key components to this script:

1. You ask a question – "Curious – are you interested in XYZ?"

2. You offer value – "If so, I have a blog post that helps you XYZ…"

3. You ask permission – "Just reply with the word YES and I'll send it over…"

4. You don't pressure them – "If you're not interested, no worries at all."

Along with being free (it doesn't cost you anything to message your 1st degree LinkedIn connections), this script is highly effective *if* you're targeting the right audience for the topic of your post, and framing up your message in terms of explaining the *benefit* they'll get by reading your content.

Social Media Posts

I utilize social media scheduling tools to share the same pieces of content every single week, promoting the same blog posts over and over again on various networks.

The reason I do this is simple - people aren't always going to see a quick status update you fire off once or twice about a great blog you wrote. So you have to continually *remind* them about this valuable piece of content. Vary the days and times you share a link to the specific blog post to try and catch people on different times on each social network, ensuring people in different time zones won't miss your post if it pops up in their feed.

I wouldn't recommend sharing a link to the same blog post every single day, but I think once or twice a week or even just a few times per month is a great way to keep it visible. You can also vary the text you use to introduce the post and link, so that it's not just a copy-and-paste update over and over again with the same words.

Have a few different updates (with different sentences) that you can rotate as you schedule and share social media status updates that link to that same blog post.

Also, as I've re-shared the status updates about the same blog post over time on social networks, I've seen people who already read it like and comment, stating that the post was really good, helpful, etc. That adds an extra layer of social proof for *new* people seeing the status update to go and check out the blog finally.

See how this works?

How To Format Your Blog Posts

Writing for an online audience is a different animal than printed books or magazines.

Especially if someone is consuming your content on a mobile device, he or she doesn't want to see huge blocks of text that go on forever.

Instead, the typical blog reader scrolls up and down, scanning and skimming for sections that catch their attention.

Break up your blog text by using lots of new paragraphs and white space. Add in subheadlines and images to break up longer sections of body copy. Not only does this help catch the eye of someone scrolling quickly through your post to find the particular section or strategy they want to cull from it, but it also makes the post more visually attractive (and thereby more "readable") in the eyes of the reader.

Use Your Words Wisely

Contrary to popular belief, there isn't necessarily a "magic" word count to aim for with your blog posts.

Depending on your audience, short-form blogs might work well, while longer-form pieces might bomb.

Personally, I try to keep my blogs between 650-850 words when I can, delivering one key tip or one quick win so that people can consume and apply the content quickly.

Sometimes I go much longer, and, like anything else, readership drops off. However, those who *do* consume your longer blog pieces also often become great sales prospects, because they're obviously digging in deeply to your materials and wanting to consume more and more as a result.

When it doubt, keep your post short and simple, delivering a few (or even just one) great nuggets and quick wins.

Write The Headline First!

As I mentioned earlier in the book, headlines are everything, and you should spend far more time focusing on crafting an irresistible headline than you should on the actual content of the blog itself.

After all, if your headline stinks, nobody will read all that great content you created anyway!

When I'm ready to pen a new blog post, I write out several different headlines based on the idea or topic of the post. And then, once I have a headline that makes me (even as the author!) think, "Wow, I'd like to know what that is!" *then* I go about writing a blog that delivers on the promise of the headline.

If you can get *yourself* excited or curious about the content of a blog post based on the headline you just created, you have a winner. Spend the rest of your time writing a post that delivers on the promised benefit your headline says it will deliver.

(Note: For all my best tips, tools and headline templates, go to https:// ContentMarketingMachine.com/Bonus)

Blog Post Framework - Follow This Template!

As I mentioned earlier in formatting most types of content, there is a specific flow and formula to crafting a compelling blog post.

It starts with the headline, and then moves into the blog summary or blog description, which is usually a sentence or two long.

This blog summary must expand upon the promise of your headline, enticing potential readers to want to read the full post.

Your blog summary text is critical, because it, along with your headline, is what typically displays on search engines, blog directories and other online areas where your posts are displayed.

Here's an example of how it looks online when you have several blog posts displayed:

The Massive Personal Branding Mistake I Discovered From Studying 16,000 LinkedIn Profiles

Discover the 1 line of your LinkedIn profile that must be pitch perfect in order to ensure your chances of success on the platform.

Continue Reading →

The Best (and Most Simple) Customer Survey Ever

This simple (yet often overlooked!) question makes selling to your ideal clients or potential customers far easier and more effective.

Continue Reading →

How To Go Viral on LinkedIn (The Answer Will Surprise You)

Given its well-earned reputation as a stuffy, "professional" platform, going viral on LinkedIn requires a counterintuitive approach.

You can see what a prominent role the blog summary sentence plays, so make sure you craft one that expands upon the curiosity, utility or benefit your headline promises.

Once you have a headline and summary sentence in place, it's time to structure the actual blog post.

Following with what I outlined earlier, you want to start with a great "hook" - an introduction that grabs the reader by his or her collar and refuses to let go.

Great hooks suck you into a story, and typically involve some sort of situation or circumstance that contains drama, curiosity or another powerful emotion.

Once you have your hook in place, you transition to what I call the "nut graph" - a succinct explanation of what the reader can expect to learn from the rest of the post.

Next up is the "body" copy - the actual guts of the post where you share your strategy, tips, etc.

Finally, you *always* want to end your blog post with a Call To Action (CTA), inviting the reader to take the next step - be it reading an additional piece of your content, contacting you to set up a free discovery call, watching a video, attending a webinar or whatever else it might be.

Your CTA should always be tied into the topic or content of your blog post, and it needs to expand upon and enhance what you've laid out already.

Benefits of Blogging

As one of the oldest forms of online content around, blogs have become a safe, trusted source of information for audiences. So much depends on your audience demographic, however, because younger generations seem to gravitate more toward the bite-sized content of social media platforms like Twitter and the visual elements of YouTube and Instagram.

Older audiences, however, "grew up" on books and blogs and still consume the written word online as a result. If *that* fits your ideal audience, then regular blogging is going to show great results for your brand and business.

Like anything else, let the marketplace dictate the results. Measure and track the effectiveness of your blog posts - especially the CTA material and links you include.

What I've found true with *my* audience is that a great blog post can serve as "cornerstone" content, meaning it's a foundational pillar of my content marketing strategy online.

A great blog post that is evergreen in its topic and strategy will deliver for years on end, driving traffic to the places you want and engaging readers to utilize your CTAs over and over again.

With that said, not every blog post can be a home run. But the more you write, and the more you pay attention and try to replicate the formula, content and style that your audience seems to engage most with, the more doubles, triples and home runs you'll hit each time you publish a new blog.

Benefits of Regular Blogging

Because blogs aren't a quick "slice of life" type of content play, they have a longer shelf life and create deeper engagement with audiences online. They can also build off each other, meaning you can do a blog series that dives deep into a particular topic, helping stitch together posts like songs on a record album.

Best of all, blogs can be repurposed into books. Whether you package up a series of themed blog posts as a compilation or just use a blog post about a specific topic to strengthen an existing book you're writing, that content can be repurposed and added into other forms of content you create.

Remember the example from earlier about my LinkedIn profile eBook that has generated so many email opt-ins and leads for me online?

It started out as a blog post, and did fine, but once I repurposed that post and packaged it up as a slick eBook in terms of formatting and images, and put it behind an email opt-in requirement, that piece of content became priceless in terms of generating ongoing leads and opt-ins for my business.

How To Blog if You Hate Writing

Here's some good news: Even if you're not Stephen King or Ernest Hemingway, you can still create (and share) quality blog posts online.

Even better, those posts can be "written" in the exact tone and voice that you use when talking to prospects about your business.

Where Speaking Meets Writing

Growing up as the son of two English professors, and later working as a journalist and author, I've been around the written word all my life.

As a result, I tend to take writing - especially in the business or marketplace setting - for granted.

For instance, many people I meet are *great* at explaining their business or how they help specific audiences when we're talking on the phone or in person.

Writing it all out, however, can be far more difficult.

Thankfully, there's a solution that makes it easy to convert your spoken words into written blog posts.

It's called transcriptions, and I've used this method for years to create transcripts for Podcasts, training videos and other audio or video materials I create and share online.

From Talking to Blogging

You can use an online transcription service (there are tons to choose from) to instantly turn you *talking* about your business or an important issue in your industry into a written blog post.

All you have to do is record yourself on your phone or computer. It doesn't have to be high-quality or fancy audio, either. Just good enough for the transcription service to understand what you're saying.

Once you've finished recording yourself, you send over your audio or video file to the transcription service, and within 24 to 72 hours they'll send you back a cleaned up, typo-free Microsoft Word document with everything you said written out.

As of this writing, online transcription rates range from $1.00 per minute to $5.00 per minute depending on how fast of a turnaround you want.

Low Cost, High Value

So how much talking do you have to do in order to create a "written" blog post?

Well, most of us speak at a rate of around 100 to 150 words per minute.

That means, if you verbally riff for 3 or 4 minutes about an issue in your industry, a tip you love giving your customers or a piece of technology you're excited about, you'll end up with a 300-600 word "written" blog post.

Ready, Set, Publish

Once you get back your transcription from the online vendor, you just need to give the document a quick proofread and edit, add in a headline and relevant links, and you've got a finished blog post ready to publish.

All for just a few dollars in most instances!

If you want to completely outsource the process, hire a freelance editor to turn your transcription into a written post, adding in subheads, editing the transcript for clarity and so on.

Not only does this transcription method for blog posts save you the time and fear of trying to "write like you talk," but many readers enjoy a blog that's written in a breezy, conversational tone as well.

Best of all, this type of "conversational" writing (and your transcript will typically read that way, like a friendly conversation) is easy to understand and makes you relatable and likable, because it showcases your true personality and communication style.

Keep in mind, too, that you can also be using that audio and video content you based your transcription around elsewhere - as a "tip of the day" video, a short podcast episode and so on.

Always find ways to take that one piece of content and repurpose it for several platforms!

Getting Visual: How To Boost Your Blog's Value

Here's an example.

Say you record a video of yourself in your office or on location talking about a specific strategy or tip. Or perhaps you recorded a podcast interview with an expert on a certain topic.

Either way, you can utilize the transcriptions of that spoken content as a written blog post, and then *also* embed the video or podcast file inside the written post too.

Whenever possible, making your blog multimedia-friendly is a good thing, because it gives your audience more choices on how to consume and engage with your content.

Someone might have gotten sucked into the blog via your headline and summary, but isn't normally a big reader. However, if he or she sees that there's a video embedded in the blog post where you explain the concept or strategy in person, that might be more appealing than reading the text itself.

It's also another opportunity for a blog reader to "see" and "hear" you face-to-face along with consuming your written content.

Remember, audio and video create a more powerful emotional bond with an audience because they literally get to "see" you face-to-face (video) and hear your voice (audio) in their heads as they engage with your post.

Blogs are Boss

Regardless of how you craft them and whether or not you add multimedia embeds inside your posts, it's worth your time to publish blogs on a regular basis. Assuming, once again, that your ideal audience consumes blog posts as part of its regular content consumption diet.

Aim for publishing one new blog every week, and then promoting the heck out of that blog all week long via the various methods (social media posts, 1-on-1 LinkedIn messages, your email list or podcast, etc.) I've discussed already.

Make it a theme if you can - write the blog post first, and then record a podcast where you talk about the strategy and idea in the blog, and let listeners know they can learn more about this topic or concept by reading the entire blog post on your site.

With blogging, consistency is key. If you can crank out 1 or 2 new blogs per week, you'll begin building momentum *and* growing a library of on-demand, easy-to-access content that you house on your website.

Even better, you can create epic blog posts that are answers to FAQs people have about you and your business.

For example, I often have Real Estate Agents contact me on LinkedIn asking how they can use the platform to find clients. So, instead of answering each inquiry individually, I say, "Great question! Here's a link to a blog post I wrote that covers that topic in depth!"

I link to a blog titled "How Real Estate Agents Can Use LinkedIn To Find Clients" and it not only gives the person the answer he or she wants, it also moves them deeper into my content funnel by offering a CTA to a free training webinar and similar lead magnets.

Blogs don't have the same star power they once carried online, but they're still a powerful form of content marketing. Make sure you don't forget to use them!

Chapter 12:
The Stream of Social

I walked to the front of the room, making sure I had everyone's undivided attention.

"Okay, I'd really like to hear your thoughts on this topic of using LinkedIn for sales," I said to the audience. "Make sure you share your thoughts and comments with me."

Then, before anyone could raise his or her hand to respond, I ran as fast I could to an exit door, leaving the room.

I waited a few moments, enjoying the nervous tension and laughter that I could hear through the closed door.

I then walked back in and went back to the front of the room.

"In real life, if we ask someone to share his or her thoughts with us, we don't usually run out of the room before he or she can answer, right?" I asked the audience. "So why do we act that way on social media?"

Here's my point: Too often on social media channels, we throw out posts asking for input or engagement, but then we "leave" the room, not bothering to engage or reply to people who do share thoughts and comments.

Here's my point: If you're going to use specific social media channels, make sure you commit to monitoring and engaging with your audience on those platforms.

Social media can be a great way to build a loyal following online *if* you put in the time and effort to engage your audience.

Keep in mind too the word "social," because far too many people are still not using the platform properly.

Bringing a Bullhorn to a Cocktail Party

In fact, it drives me bonkers when I see people using social media platforms like an extension of TV, print or radio advertising, blasting out one-sided offers and sales pitches.

Interruption-based advertising has been the norm here in the United States for the past century, but it's time is over.

So instead of using social media channels to "interrupt" people with one-sided, promotional offers they didn't ask for, you must find ways to create engagement and brand affinity with the content you create and share.

Think of it this way: Nobody walks into a cocktail party and interrupts everyone else by shouting through a bullhorn, "Hey, who needs help building their website? I've got a great offer going right now …"

Instead, you *socialize.* You share stories. You ask questions. You engage with people in conversations.

In short, you share life and build relationships.

That is the secret sauce behind successful social media content.

What Platforms To Use

Rather than focusing on a ton of specific platforms, some of which will change or be outdated by the time you read these words, I'd rather focus on an overall strategy based around who your target audience is *and* your favorite ways to communicate.

Above all else, you must decide what networks *your* ideal audience spends the most time on. And then you need to go all-in on creating original content, sharing it on those platforms and engaging with those who begin paying attention to you as a result.

Most important, you want to play to your strengths and communication style. If you're great on camera and love talking, make sure you're delivering a heavy dose of video content. If you love using a "day in the life" type image or selfie of you on location somewhere to illustrate a lesson or strategy, then go heavy on that approach. If you prefer writing pithy quotes or sharing thoughts around an invaluable lesson you've learned, that's fine too.

Bite-Sized is Best

Keep in mind that with *most* social networks, shorter is better. Bite-sized content rules the day, from status updates to videos and everything else. People's attention spans are shorter than ever, and they're also more distracted than ever.

Get right to the point with your posts, and remember the same principles I've already outlined of what goes into quality content: Tell great stories. Be visual. Make sure your audience *feels* something. Share your personality. Be unique. Ask questions and engage when someone responds.

Where is Your Audience?

Knowing *where* your audience hangs out online is critical to crafting a solid social media strategy.

For me, it's easy: Because I provide a B2B service (online training courses for professionals) LinkedIn is where I spend almost all my time, effort and energy.

For you, it might be a different platform. But here's my point: Put the lion's share of your time, effort and attention into the 1 or 2 platforms your ideal audience uses most. It's fine to have a secondary strategy of also posting on other networks (for instance, I still post content on Facebook and Twitter), but you should never lose sight of those networks that are most important to your audience.

Also, don't try and have a presence on every single social network under the sun. Instead, focus on being really, really active on the 2-3 networks where you'll reach the vast majority of your audience.

Otherwise, you'll be chasing every hot new network, posting a bunch of content, not staying engaged, consistent or committed, and then getting frustrated and giving up as a result.

The Big Kids Table - Facebook and LinkedIn

Here's an interesting trend: If you look at the larger, more established social networks, such as Facebook and LinkedIn, you'll see that they are trying to be "everything to everyone" in terms of the type of content you can create and share on their platform.

Facebook in particular does a good job of studying smaller, niche social networks that spring up (such as Instagram a few years back), and then either buying them outright or mimicking and copying that platform's features directly into Facebook.

LinkedIn, although it moves much slower, does the same thing, only aiming at a B2B audience instead of B2C like Facebook does.

Another generational trend I've noticed with social media is that younger audiences (teens and pre-teens) tend to flock to newer, niche networks, leaving "old people" to use the more established platforms like LinkedIn or Facebook.

Then, once those niche networks become mainstream enough, older users jump on too, followed by marketers and businesses, and that platform starts getting commercialized and monetized as a result. Finally, bigger platforms like Facebook and LinkedIn copy its core features and roll out their own versions. The kids then leave and the adults stay, because what teenager wants to be on the same social network as mom or grandma?

Paid Social Media

Confession time: I've spent tens of thousands of dollars on Facebook Ads and gotten terrible results. I've written my own ads and hired others to write them. I've used video and text. I've used images. I've hired three different Facebook ad agencies and done ads on my own. And nothing has worked.

So don't look for me to wave my pom-poms as the top cheerleader for paid social media advertising.

What I've seen work far better is personalized, 1-on-1 engagement that happens at the human level, meaning I'm not "interrupting" someone's stream with a paid ad, but rather reaching out directly to connect and then engaging back-and-forth with the other person.

Now, that doesn't mean paid ads don't work. In fact, you can't scroll for more than a few seconds without someone in your newsfeed talking about how he or she is living on a yacht and making millions thanks to Facebook Ads.

My only advice here is go in with your eyes open. Ads *can* work, but it's important to consider the *context* of the relationships they create with a client or prospect as a result.

When I hear someone interviewed on my favorite podcast, for example, and that person *demonstrates* real authority and expertise, *and* I enjoy his or her communication style and personality, the *context* of our relationship is much stronger than if I'd clicked on a random ad that this person posted on Facebook.

The same is true of other forms of content marketing. When you read someone's book or blog post, his or her *content* creates a powerful *context* for your relationship moving forward.

With that in mind, an effective ad should always be directing someone to your best (and free) content, not an offer. Remember the elements I've already covered in this book, and how your social media content must become the *currency* you use to "buy" someone's time and attention on each platform.

What Great Social Media Content Looks Like

When it comes to putting together an effective social media post, think in terms of *utility* and *empathy.*

What I mean by *utility* is offering something practical or useful to your ideal audience - perhaps a quick anecdote or lesson that links to a longer piece of content to help them solve a problem or achieve a goal.

When I say *empathy,* I'm talking about sharing enough of the "real" you so that people can empathize with you at a human level, thereby beginning to *know* and *like* you more as a result.

For instance, sharing a "day in the life" post about you taking the afternoon off to play with your kids at the park reminds your audience that you're a family person, just like them, and that their priorities align with yours.

Or maybe it's going on a travel adventure, a photo of you doing your favorite hobby or sharing a personal story of an obstacle overcome.

Whatever it is, the more you can share your "real" life without being melodramatic or phony, the more people will feel bonded to you emotionally. And once people develop an emotional affinity for your personal brand, doing business with you becomes much easier.

For instance, I referenced my Business Coach John Michael Morgan earlier. Just the other day, John shared on Facebook the story of how he danced in his young daughter's recital despite being terrified of doing it. John tied that story (complete with a video of him dancing on stage among pint-sized ballerinas) into a lesson on the importance of overcoming fear in life and business.

In one simple post, he not only built *empathy* ("Oh, look, what a great dad!"), but also added some *utility* (Overcoming and pushing through your greatest fears, and the reward that lies on the other side).

Anytime you can mix those two elements into a powerful story that also showcases your personal brand, you have the makings of a powerful social media post.

Pull People Away from the Platform

The most important note I can end this chapter with is the reminder that all social networks are rented land, meaning you don't get to make the rules or dictate the terms of engagement.

As a result, you should *always* be angling for ways to get someone *off* a particular social network and onto your email list, website or the telephone instead.

Yes, you want to use the distribution methods and relationship tools that social networks provide, but you *never* want to become overly reliant on any one network to fully house your audience and all the resulting engagements you have.

For instance, nearly every LinkedIn status update or 1-on-1 message I send aims to get people *off* LinkedIn and over to a landing page or blog post housed on my website.

Remember, the social networks give, and they can take away. At any moment, your favorite platform can start charging you higher rates, restrict or remove your favorite features or anything else they want to do. Remember, it's their digital sandbox, and they own everything inside it.

Whenever you create and share content via social media, always find a way to focus on moving people over to your website and building your email list so that *you* control the relationship with a new prospect moving forward.

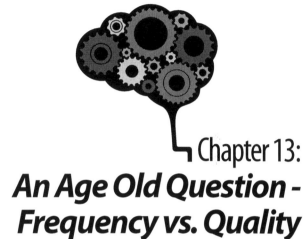

Chapter 13:
An Age Old Question -
Frequency vs. Quality

"Uh, I don't know anything about that industry."

"Well, Nemo, looks you're going to become the expert on it today."

That was my introduction back in 1999 to the wild world of working for *The Associated Press,* one of the world's largest news gathering and distribution networks.

With a global operation covering nearly every inhabited place on planet earth, the AP was expected to crank out original stories *and* curate the most important local news of the day in what initially felt like impossibly tight daily deadlines. This applied to every bureau all over the world, and in our location (Minneapolis-St. Paul) there was never a shortage of news to cover, aggregate and distribute via print and radio newswires.

For me, that meant becoming an "instant expert" on whatever popped up that day on the news side. It also meant churning out as many "straight to the point" or "just the facts" type stories as quickly as possible.

I became a content creation machine during my years at the AP, and to this day I credit that training for my ability to turn any subject into readable prose in a quick and effective fashion.

When it comes to content marketing, however, frequency is not always your friend.

Quality is.

I've said it before and I'll say it again: I'd much rather you put out fewer pieces of content and make them higher quality.

The reason is simple: With today's never-ending stream of content to choose from online, you might only get one chance to impress someone. What if the only piece of content someone sees from you is a half-baked, rushed-to-publish blog post that doesn't showcase your best work?

More importantly, quality content sets you apart from the competition in a way nothing else can.

In his wonderful book *Deep Work,* Cal Newport argues this point quite well:

"Deep work is valuable because the impacts of the digital network revolution cut both ways. If you can create something useful, its reachable audience (e.g., employers or customers) is essentially limitless - which greatly magnifies your reward," he writes. "On the other hand, if what you're producing is mediocre, then you're in trouble, as it's too easy for your audience to find a better alternative online.

"To succeed you have to produce the absolute best stuff you're capable of producing—a task that requires depth."

What To Aim For

Try to create and share 1-2 pieces of truly *great* content each week. Whether it's a blog post, podcast episode, training video or whatever else, pour your absolute *best* effort into that content.

(Note: This doesn't mean each piece of content has to be in-depth, dense or long. Rather, it just needs to be high-quality and of value to your ideal audiences.)

Over time, those pieces of content will build upon each other like stones comprising the wall of a castle, helping fortify your content marketing efforts over the longer term.

In the shorter term, supplement those "quality" pieces of content you create each week with shorter, "day in the life" type status updates or quick anecdotes that make for good social media fodder.

Frequency, as you're about to see, does indeed matter.

Where Frequency Pays Off

Bestselling Author and Speaker Gary Vaynerchuk is one of the best content marketers on the planet. He literally built himself up from an unknown twenty-something kid working the floor inside his father's New Jersey-based liquor store to a globally-recognized entrepreneur, author and keynote speaker purely on passion, engagement and nonstop hustle.

With millions of followers across several social media platforms, Gary now spends his days with a camera crew following him everywhere he goes, documenting his business meetings, speeches, phone calls and other parts of his professional day.

Gary's team then turns all that raw content into polished blog posts, videos, podcasts, photos and other forms of content that is shared online.

Think about it: The guy *literally* records, edits and shares the best parts of his day across multiple different platforms and content types. And he does it *every single day* … talk about frequency in action!

I'm not suggesting you hire a camera crew to follow and share your every professional move like Gary does. Rather, use his extreme approach as motivation to share more of *your* day via quick bites of content you can create and share online.

For example, you can snap a quick selfie before you go onstage to give a talk, delivering a subtle reminder to your online audience that you're a credible, in-demand public speaker and presenter.

You can also utilize a social media scheduling tool to ensure your previous content stays in a rotation, re-sharing older, evergreen pieces of content that someone might have missed when you'd initially posted it.

The more you can stay in front of people online (frequency), the more you remain top-of-mind and familiar as a potential business partner or vendor someone might want to utilize.

That doesn't mean spamming people and platforms with the same three pieces of content every single day, but rather mixing and matching older content (dressing it up with a fresh description or photo, as one example) with newer, original "day in the life" posts, photos or anecdotes.

Social media scheduling tools also make it easy to share, track and then re-share your online content across multiple platforms.

Again, frequency is important, and you need to find a rhythm for what you can share and how often to share it each week.

But even more, *quality* carries the day.

If Gary Vaynerchuk didn't create *quality* content, he could livestream his entire day and nobody would watch. But because he combines *quality* and *quantity*, Gary rules the roost when it comes to successful content marketing.

Take that as a dose of inspiration as you craft your own plan of attack.

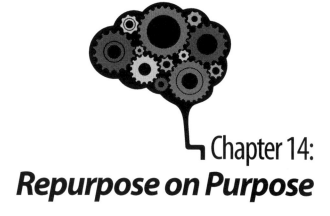

Chapter 14:
Repurpose on Purpose

One of the biggest challenges in content marketing is squeezing as much online mileage as you possibly can from each piece of content you create.

That means embracing the role of repurposing your content across multiple channels, formats and platforms. And, thanks to technology, it's become easier than ever to accomplish.

Here's an example of how this might work: Say you shoot a short video (2-3 minutes long) of yourself sharing some of your best strategies that help your ideal audience solve a core problem they have.

Now, you can take and edit (if needed) that video, then upload it as a "native" video across several platforms - YouTube, Facebook, LinkedIn and so on.

Next, you can send over your video file link to an online transcription service, and within a few hours to a few days (depending on how fast you want it back) you'll get back a typo-free transcription of what you had to say for just a few dollars. (As of this writing, most services only charge a few dollars for each minute of transcribed audio or video content.)

With some quick edits (adding headlines and subheads, formatting, etc.) you now have a *written* piece of content to publish as an original blog post across various social media platforms and on your own website.

Now, you go back to the video you originally shot and edited, strip out the audio and upload it as an audio podcast on iTunes and other platforms.

Finally, you grab a still image from the video or find a separate stock image to illustrate the strategies you were teaching, and throw that image up on photo sharing networks, along with some text, linking back to the full audio, video and/or written blog post.

Even better, you can embed the full video and/or podcast episode right into your written blog post, giving people multiple ways to consume your content.

As a final step, you can utilize the headline and "nut graph" summary of your blog post as the basis for a blast message to send to your email subscribers, pointing them to the blog post, which also includes the audio and video embedded directly within it.

All of that coming from a quick 2-3 minute video you shot on your iPhone!

Give The Audience Options

This is why repurposing is so powerful and so important - it takes one piece of content and expands it across multiple channels, platforms and communication styles in a matter of minutes.

The more you can give your online audience multiple formats to consume your content in (audio, video, written, image-based, etc.) the more you'll satisfy *their* preferred ways of consuming your valuable content. That means deeper engagement, better reach and more sales as a result.

183 / Chapter FOURTEEN

Hear me well, Dear Reader: Never, *ever,* create a single piece of content without thinking, "How else can I repurpose this? What other channels or platforms can I share it on?"

Again, the easiest way to do this is to *start* with video (either you alone on camera, behind the camera showing something on your computer or even interviewing an expert via a video chat or call).

Once you have some video, then it's super easy to strip out and utilize the audio for a podcast.

It's also quite easy to take that stripped out audio or even the entire video file and upload it to an online transcription service so you can get back a written document for a blog post.

Repurposing your content like this becomes the foundation for a steady stream of content across multiple platforms and channels, which is critical to ensure your online audiences can consume your content using *their* favorite channels or communication styles.

(Note: Visit https://ContentMarketingMachine.com/Bonus to get a list of all my favorite repurposing tools and software programs.)

How it Works

Here's an example I just did the other day.

We'd just moved into a new home, and the trash piled up in our garage looked like Mount Everest. I called our garbage hauler, only to find out they'd charge me *$10 per extra bag of garbage* I had outside of the can they'd given us.

That would have been more than my mortgage payment, so I called the local dump and found out I could unload up to 500 pounds of garbage for only $30 total.

Done!

I loaded up our minivan with trash (best use I've found for it to date ... remember my story about spending $35k to feel emasculated?) and sped off to the dump.

It was 95 degrees and humid, and as I unloaded heaps of refuse from the back of our minivan, flies swirled around me in the heat. Huge bulldozers moved mounds of trash into enormous piles nearby.

Driving home, I did something I often do - decided to turn a life experience into a piece of content.

I thought about the symbol of a garbage dump, and how so often in our heads we have tons of mental "trash" that stinks up our thinking and limits our ability to grow and succeed.

I knew I had a good *story* (the trash dump experience) to encode my *lesson* (the importance of clearing out your mental "trash") inside of.

So I recorded a podcast, starting with the trash dump story as my "hook" and then riffing about my own mental trash and how I've tried to clear my head of it. I also mentioned a book called *Psycho Cybernetics* from the 1950s that, despite it's goofy title, is super helpful in improving your mindset and clearing mental hurdles. I also thought of a great line my Business Coach (John Michael Morgan) taught me that tied all of this content to business and sales - *Income improvement follows self-improvement.*

I came up with a headline - *The "Psycho" Garbage Dump Story That Will Help You Increase Sales.*

Next I wrote up a summary sentence: *It was a smelly, stinky adventure, but it reminded me of the core secret to selling more of anything, along with becoming more successful in business (and life).*

Next, I flipped that Podcast headline and description into a blast email I sent to my list:

Subject line: *worst smell ever*

Email copy: *Yes, it was awful, but it reminded me of the core secret of selling more of anything, along with becoming more successful in business (and life).*

It happened the other day during a trip to the local garbage dump, and I "aired out" the whole misadventure in this new episode of the Nemo Radio Podcast --

LISTEN: The "Psycho" Garbage Dump Story That Will Help You Increase Sales

You should be glad you weren't along for the ride as I unloaded heaps of trash, but you will want to implement the critical mindset lesson the experience reminded me of.

Talk more soon!

To extend the story, I can take the transcript of the podcast (which was 20 minutes long) and turn that into an eBook on improving your mindset. Since I spoke for so long, that transcript will end up being a few thousand words at least - perfect for an eBook.

Take Advantage of the Tools

There are lots of tools you can use to make repurposing your content fast and easy, and it's critical that you do.

Remember, you want to give people opportunities to consume your content in as many different formats and styles as possible, so be purposeful about repurposing!

Chapter 15:
All Systems Go: Calendars and Strategic Planning

To this point, I've covered so much of what goes into creating engaging content.

Now, we need to organize it all!

Being a self-employed and creative person, I loathe feeling tethered to a calendar or set schedule. At the same time, I've found that without some sort of structure and strategy, I don't produce and promote original content like I should.

So, once you decide on what types of content you want to create, share and promote on a regular basis, it's time to put together a system and a calendar to make sure it gets done.

Chunk it up

As a content creator, you are officially what Cal Newport (author of *Deep Work*) calls a "knowledge worker," meaning you are taking what's in your head (knowledge) and using it to (eventually) sell your products and services.

In order to translate all that brainpower of yours into creative, engaging content, you need to block out long, uninterrupted chunks of time on your calendar each week.

In today's world, distractions are nonstop. Our iPhones have us panting like Pavlov's dogs every time a new notification pops up. In addition, the addictive nature of constantly checking social media, email and news websites fractures your ability to concentrate and perform what Newport refers to as *Deep Work*.

"Deep Work [is] professional activities performed in a state of distraction-free concentration that push your cognitive capabilities to their limit," Newport writes. "These efforts create new value, improve your skill, and are hard to replicate. Deep work is necessary to wring every last drop of value out of your current intellectual capacity."

Newport goes on to quote Author Neal Stephenson: "If I organize my life in such a way that I get lots of long, consecutive, uninterrupted time-chunks, I can write novels. [If I instead get interrupted a lot] what replaces it? Instead of a novel that will be around for a long time ... there are a bunch of e-mail messages that I have sent out to individual persons."

You might not need to write a novel, but if you want to put together a coherent and creative piece of original content, you *must* chunk your time and discipline yourself in such a way that you eliminate all distractions and just *create* for a few uninterrupted hours several times a week.

Speaking of the infinite distractions that have us bouncing back and forth online like a jumping bean, Newport writes, "this state of fragmented attention cannot accommodate deep work, which requires long periods of uninterrupted thinking.

"Deep thinking, such as forming a new business strategy or writing an important [piece of content], get fragmented into distracted dashes that produce muted quality.

"To make matters worse for depth, there's increasing evidence that this shift toward the shallow is not a choice that can be easily reversed. Spend enough time in a state of frenetic shallowness and you *permanently* reduce your capacity to perform deep work."

Thanks, Cal - you're an absolute fountain of positivity!

This next line from Newport's book is so important I'm going to quote it for the second time in our journey together: "Deep work is valuable because the impacts of the digital network revolution cut both ways. If you can create something useful, its reachable audience (e.g., employers or customers) is essentially limitless - which greatly magnifies your reward. On the other hand, if what you're producing is mediocre, then you're in trouble, as it's too easy for your audience to find a better alternative online.

"To succeed you have to produce the absolute best stuff you're capable of producing—a task that requires depth."

Personally, I find I have the most creative juice and clearest mind in the mornings, so I block out those hours for creative time. During those stretches, I do my best not to check email, social media or anything else. (If I do, I invariably get distracted by or stressed from some situation that's popped up related to my business.)

Then, in the afternoon, I log into social media, email and news sites to see what I've missed. Those engagements are much more shallow and easier to move back and forth between, so it works well to wind down my day handling those elements of my business. In addition, crafting and creating some quality content to begin your day helps you feel like you've accomplished something important and significant. (Which you have!)

Scheduling Time to Feed Your Mind

It was not the answer I expected, but I have no doubt it would have made my parents smile.

I'd just emerged from an incredible 48 hours spent inside a hotel meeting room with some of the most successful entrepreneurs, authors, and creative minds in today's marketplace.

And what emerged was a common thread, a common passion that seemed like a burning fire in the pit of each person's belly.

The Big Reveal

They talked about it over and over, in various ways and forms, but it was the common thread that made all these people in the room the most successful people in their respective industries.

It was something my parents (both English teachers) had tried to teach me from an early age, as I grew up in a home where the basement was literally lined from floor-to-ceiling with books.

So the big reveal, the common ingredient to the wild success of all the great minds in the room surrounding me, was …

Books.

Lots of books.

Some of these guys read as many as five books a week!

"If I'm not spending at least two hours a day reading, I'm going to have withdrawal," said Dan Miller, the bestselling author of *48 Days To The Work You Love.*

Ray Edwards, a top copywriter whose clients include Tony Robbins, talked about the critical role books have played both in his mindset and in building a successful online business.

Nigel Green, who helped grow a healthcare sales company from $94 million to $350 million of revenue in 36 months, told me he devours the biographies of great leaders from all walks of life.

Give Yourself Permission

What stunned me most was how free everyone in that room was at giving himself permission to read as part of his "job."

In my own work, I've always felt guilty reading books (even business books!) during "work" hours, or somehow believed I wasn't being productive.

Yet it was made clear to me during those 48 hours that the reason each person in that room was so successful was because of reading, learning and (most important) applying the lessons learned in all of those books.

Needless to say, I've changed my ways, and now start my day by reading.

Reading a great book to begin your day is a fantastic method for turning on and tuning up the creative centers of your brain before you jump into content creation.

Along with giving you inspiration and ideas for your own content, reading puts you into a creative place and revs up your storytelling engine as well.

(For a list of my favorite business books, go to https://ContentMarketingMachine. com/Bonus)

You've Created - Now What?

Once you've made time in your calendar for reading and creating content in a distraction-free space, it's time to figure out a publishing and promotion schedule.

This is important, because you want to train your audience as to *when* they can expect to see new content from you showing up on certain channels.

You also want to try and spread out the different *types* of content you publish so that they hit on certain days of the week.

For instance, if you publish a podcast, make sure new episodes come out on the same day and time each week. On days when you're not publishing a podcast, have a new blog post or video go up.

Also, depending on your target audience and what online platforms they utilize most, you'll want to try and time *when* your content goes live on each platform to catch them on those networks.

For example, since the vast majority of my potential clients use LinkedIn, I publish a lot of content on there during work hours (9:00 a.m. to 5:00 p.m.), especially in the middle of the week (Tuesday, Wednesday Thursday) since those are the times of heaviest use on the platform.

For you, it might be a different audience on a different network. Either way, it's very important to know *which* networks you want to focus on, and then make sure you're consistently creating and sharing *quality* content on those platforms.

Remember, you don't need to be active on *every* social network. Instead, you just need to be on the ones where the vast majorities of your ideal audiences are.

Scheduling Posts

One great way to streamline the entire process of posting on social media is to utilize social media scheduling tools and calendar apps like Buffer or Hootsuite. These types of tools not only schedule and post all your content across numerous social networks, but also *analyze* the results.

Buffer, for example, will analyze all of my content sharing across multiple platforms, then report back to me which posts get the most engagement on which networks, including the time of day people most engaged with my content, the best days of the week, etc. As a result, Buffer comes up with a suggested weekly calendar (days and times) when I should post content on each specific network based on the results I'm getting to that point using my own dates and times.

With social media scheduling tools, it's important to track the analytics and see which pieces of content create engagement, and *when* they create engagement. That way, you can create more of the same content and schedule it to go live at the best possible times based on past performance.

Lastly, many social media scheduling tools like Buffer allow you to reshare (or re-Buffer) popular posts over and over, saving you time from having to copy, paste and repost the same piece of content again and again.

Take advantage of these re-sharing tools to keep your core lead magnets (free eBooks, video trainings, webinars, etc.) front and center on social media channels each week, along with analyzing and re-sharing popular pieces of content (blog posts, videos, etc.) again and again over time to keep their momentum going.

As for how often to re-post certain pieces of popular content, I have no issue re-sharing a popular and evergreen piece of content (blog post, training video, etc.) 2-3 times per month, varying the days and times to try and catch different audiences in different time zones.

I also schedule my various lead magnets (webinars, eBooks, etc.) to go out one a day across various social networks, again varying the times to try and catch audiences in different time zones.

As long as you are mixing in enough *new and original* content with older posts and lead magnets you re-share, you'll have the balance you need to make the most of your social media scheduling.

The Lifecycle of a Piece of Content

Here's an example of how to get the most mileage out of a single piece of content.

Once I publish a new blog post or podcast episode, I'll share it that day on social media networks and via a blast to my email list.

I'll also schedule some additional social media posts to go out 1-2 days later, sharing that same piece of content one or two more times across different platforms and different channels. I'll vary the time of day I share to try and catch audiences in different time zones and parts of the world.

Next, I'll measure how that content performed in terms of page views on my website or blog, clicks on social media and overall engagement (comments, shares, etc.).

If a post seems like it was a hit, I'll schedule it go out on my social media platforms again 1-2 weeks later, and then again 30 days or so after that.

And, based on *that* performance, I might again set up some repeat shares of that same post a few more times in the months to come (perhaps sharing it 2-3 times per month for the next 3 months).

In addition, about once a week I'll go back through my blog archives and re-share older posts (via Buffer or another tool) that I haven't promoted in a long time. I look for content that is still relevant (not tied to a specific news story or current event) enough to re-share, and this helps me sprinkle in some valuable content my online audiences either missed the first time around or weren't around to discover yet. (Keep in mind you're always adding new followers and online audience members each day, and those people aren't necessarily going to go back and read the past 12 months of blog posts or watch all the training videos you've created.)

The bottom line is, like a hit song on the radio, you want to keep your top-performing content in regular rotation. Make sure you're re-sharing it a few times per month, and also re-sharing your best lead magnets on an almost daily basis.

Doing that, plus diving back into your blog, video or podcast archives to re-share older posts from months ago gives you enough variety to keep your social media stream from looking like the same 3-4 items on blast repeat. (Especially if you're always adding in new and original posts each week based around the fresh content you're creating.)

Pay Attention to Linguistic Styles and Network-Specific Nuance

Remember too that when formatting content to share across multiple social networks, there is a unique tone and communication style for each one. That means you need to customize the text of your content one way for Twitter and another way for Facebook. And yet another way for LinkedIn. Each platform has its own subtle nuances, jargon and "vibe" that should be taken into consideration.

I'm not saying you have to spend hours customizing each post for each network, but also don't fall into the "one size fits all" approaching of copying and pasting the exact same text for every single social network when sharing a new post.

Crafting a Content Calendar

Depending on how long it takes you to turn around and publish a piece of content, you will want to schedule out your week to allow time for creating, publishing and promoting each piece of content you create.

Again, it all depends upon what type of content you want to focus on creating and sharing most, and also what times of day work best for you to be at your creative best.

As I mentioned earlier, I have a general rule of thumb where I keep my mornings open for creating, publishing and promoting content. Afternoons are left for answering emails, checking social media and so on.

I also batch all my 1-on-1 and group coaching calls for the same day each week, enabling me to keep my mind, voice and thoughts as uncluttered as possible for the rest of the time.

Protect Your Time!

Using an online calendar tool has saved me immense time and stress while also ensuring I provide openings for client calls and phone time as needed.

I use a simple program called Calendly (there are tons to choose from) that connects online to my main Google Calendar.

So anything I book on my Google Calendar (from taking my son to a baseball game to a doctor appointment to reading time in the morning) gets shown as "unavailable" on Calendly.

Whatever slots I leave *open* on my Google Calendar, Calendly allows people online to book for coaching calls or something else involving my 1-on-1 time and attention.

You can also set times of day for when to accept appointments, build space between engagements and even take payments with online calendar programs like Calendly.

Whatever method or tool you use, it's critical to block out your time online! If you can, leave one day a week open for random calls, client engagements or whatever else, but *protect* the rest of your calendar!

That way, when someone asks for your time, you can just give him or her a link to your online calendar, and he or she has to adjust to *your* schedule, rather than creating a hodgepodge or random appointments you book on a whim when someone calls or emails.

In addition, scheduling and seeing your time visually with an online calendar helps you commit to the process of the tasks you've put in front of yourself to accomplish.

Scheduling Your Content Lifecycle

Just as important is knowing how much time to schedule for what I call the "lifecycle" for each piece of content you create.

For example, right now I'm making podcasting a priority, publishing two new episodes per week. I publish new episodes every Tuesday and Thursday morning, and then promote each episode via social media posts and a blast message to my email list.

With the recording and podcasting software I use, I can batch record several episodes all at once, then schedule them to go "live" on various podcasting networks on a specific day and time. I can also pre-schedule social media posts and email blasts as well.

The key for me is knowing what pieces of content are supposed to go live on what days, and then working backward from there.

For example, if I know I need a new podcast episode going live on Tuesday and then again on Thursday, I typically block out Monday morning to record, edit and schedule both episodes, along with writing copy to promote each episode via social media and email blasts. Typically in those 4 hours of Monday morning I can get all of that done, assuming I'm not getting distracted answering emails, checking social media and so on.

Keep Space Open for Creativity!

As much as you need to set and maintain a rigid online calendar for your content creation and promoting efforts, you also want to leave windows open for creativity and inspiration.

Here's a perfect example. Just this morning, I ran across this old photo of my dad playing with us when I was around 2 years old:

Something about the image struck me, and I decided at first just to journal a bit about it with a quick post on Facebook and LinkedIn.

Here's what I put on Facebook:

Next, I took the same photo and expanded my thoughts a bit on LinkedIn:

Now, with my thoughts more fully forming, I decided to write a blast email *and* tie it into my LinkedIn Riches online course as well.

Here's what the email looked like:

(Subject Line): *such a powerful photo*

(Email Body):

My father died when I was 17.

This grainy photo from 1977 captures in one chaotic moment where his focus was most nights:

What I remember (and what is eternal) was his character and his choice to spend time pouring into the lives of his kids vs. chasing career ambitions.

Kids spell "love" T-I-M-E and it's a major reason I work from home and shape my schedule around our family life (not the other way around).

I would give anything for more time with my dad, and it impacted me profoundly that he was always home around 4pm every day and available for me on weekends too.

In today's online era, there is literally no excuse not to do work you love and shape your work schedule around your family (not the other way around).

If you find yourself reading this on yet another Monday morning where you're miserable at work and missing your family, then let's do something about it!

Back in 2012, I worked a "safe" day job that paid me six figures and had great benefits.

And I was miserable.

I used to drive home each evening listening to the song "Moving Backwards" by Ben Rector, daydreaming about a time when I'd walk into my boss' office and say the opening words to the song:

I saw you there and looked you straight between the eyes and said, "I'm leaving."

One day, I finally did.

When I quit that "safe" day job, I had one client, enough money for 30 days and a stay-at-home wife and three young boys depending on me.

It wasn't a "safe" situation. I didn't have investors or a huge pile of cash to fall back on.

What I did have, however, was a plan - using the Internet (LinkedIn in particular) to find, engage and sell to my ideal clients.

I share the entire story on this webinar:

Free Training: How To Generate Unlimited Leads + Add Clients in ANY Niche using LinkedIn!

[Note: I made the text above a hyperlink to the webinar: https://linkedinriches.com/join]

One thing I'd discovered watching my dad in the 17 years we had together was that he didn't play it safe with life. He dared to be great and dream big.

So I decided I would, too.

So after quitting that "safe" day job back in 2012, I'm still standing, six years later, writing you this note from my home office.

Regardless of whether you ever want to work with me directly inside one of my online courses or via 1-on-1 coaching, my challenge to you is this ...

Build your work around your family life - not the other way around.

The impact of this will long outlive your work-related accomplishments, as evidenced by the photo I shared above.

Sound like a plan?

Good.

Now let's make it happen!

- John Nemo

Next, I decided to record a podcast episode riffing off the copy and main themes from the email.

I recorded the podcast, titled it "The Critical Life (and Work) Lesson Captured in a Photo from 1977" and used the email copy as the Podcast description text.

Finally, I saved the email copy and some headline ideas inside my project management software (Basecamp) so I could expand it into a blog post to publish on my website and LinkedIn later today or sometime this week.

If I hadn't built into my calendar the ability to have a creative period open this morning, I might have missed all of that content. Notice too how I started small, with a quick photo and a few words on Facebook, and how, when I decided to again share the photo on LinkedIn, I had more thoughts, and then, by the time I decided to write the email, I had enough copy to put together a good story that also tied to a business lesson that would resonate with my audience.

Finally, while I was immersed in this idea and the story behind it, I hit "record" on a new podcast episode to capture my thoughts.

This is critical, and something you'll discover as you create content. When you feel it, capture it!

Don't just jot down the idea and promise yourself you'll come back to it later. Drop everything and *do* the work. Having a rigid-yet-flexible calendar is a great way to build in spaces for that type of work to flourish. It is so, so important to take those creative juices that bubble up in a specific moment and run with them!

Scheduling = Sanity

You need to find your own rhythm and ideal strategy for creating, sharing and promoting your content. It can be as varied as you like, and there's no hard and fast or set rules you must follow.

The key is just to *have* some sort or strategy and some sort of schedule to follow, and then adjust as needed.

I've laid out how I make it work in this chapter, but what works for me might not be right for you.

Either way, put your best strategy and calendar down, give it a go and adjust as needed!

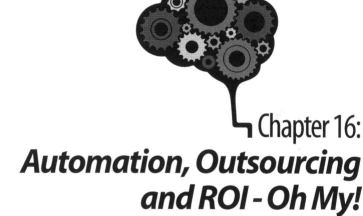

Chapter 16:
Automation, Outsourcing and ROI - Oh My!

The sky was as blue as I'd ever seen.

As we soared in a parachute hundreds of feet into the air, the ocean floor below became smaller and smaller.

My wife and I were parasailing in the Gulf of Mexico, and the view was extraordinary:

While I was gazing down on the most beautiful ocean landscape I'd ever seen, automation tools were delivering my content to a global audience online.

Emails, social media updates, blog posts, podcasts … it was all happening while I was sitting up somewhere in the Mexico sky.

That is the power of automation and the incredible technological era we live in.

Tools of the Trade

There's an ever-changing array of automation tools that allow you to streamline your content creation, scheduling and sharing process. As such, it's hard to dive too deeply into specific tools in this space because they change so often.

However, I'll hit on the *types* of tools you'll want to employ for automation purposes, and you can find my favorite and most up-to-date list of software and tools online at https://ContentMarketingMachine.com/Bonus.

Protecting Your Time

I mentioned it earlier, but getting an online calendar tool is a great first step to taking control of your schedule and ensuring you'll have the chunks of time you need to create incredible content.

An online calendar tool (I currently use Calendly) also protects your time by forcing others to find an open spot on your schedule, instead of going back and forth with several emails or calls and comparing times and dates.

The automation element of online calendar tools saves you time from manually booking appointments, along with automatically sending you email and calendar reminders closer to the actual event.

Work your Plan

I'm a big fan of Basecamp as a project management and delegation software. It allows me to stay organized, both in terms of jotting down and expanding on content ideas along with messaging members of my virtual team. Best of all, Basecamp gives you the ability to assign specific tasks to specific team members, including due dates, notifications of when the work is done, automatic reminders, integrated mobile apps and so on.

Basecamp is also very user friendly and flexible depending on what you need done. For example, when I'm assigning my Virtual Assistant (VA) a new task related to posting content on LinkedIn, I'll first record a screen capture video showing (and telling) her what I need done.

Next, I'll embed the video into a Basecamp assignment (called a "To Do") that also includes bulleted, step-by-step instructions, due dates, links to additional resources and more. If my VA has questions, she can message me right inside of the "To Do" area, and I get an immediate notification, then reply back with my answer. The entire conversation is contained within the context of the assignment, meaning she has a running dialogue to refer back to as she works through the project.

Speak it into Existence

As I referred to earlier, SpeechPad and similar transcription services make it easy to take spoken audio or video and turn it into a written piece of content.

Having spent the early part of my career as a print newspaper reporter used to transcribing taped interviews, I cannot tell you how much time and energy automated transcription services will save you.

In addition to getting back transcriptions that can be used as the basis for written blog posts or eBooks, you can also order video captions as part of the process.

With the explosion and ubiquity of online video, adding captions to *all* of your videos makes great sense and also can improve SEO.

Can You Spare a Minute?

Another interesting tool that I recently came across is called SpareMin. I'm sure there are (or will be) similar tools and software programs just like it, because the concept is genius.

You take a recorded audio file (perhaps a 30 or 60 second teaser for your next podcast episode), upload it directly into SpareMin, and it creates a ready-made video file for you, including on-screen text captions based on your audio file, stock images based on specific words in your script, transitions between slides, and more.

SpareMin does its best to automate the entire setup, so all you have to do is make any tweaks (swapping out a photo, for instance, that you don't want or editing a piece of the caption text) you desire and then grab the video file.

Now you can upload little video "trailers" for your next podcast episode to YouTube, Facebook and other platforms, linking back to your main podcast itself or the episode page online.

You can also just directly narrate audio straight into SpareMin, allowing you to create audio-based video trailers on the fly.

(Note: To see how I use SpareMin and similar tools, go to https://ContentMarketingMachine.com/Bonus)

Animated Exchanges

Speaking of video, another favorite tool I've come across is called VideoMakerFX.

It allows you to utilize pre-made, template-based animated "explainer" videos that follow a specific theme. (Real Estate, Software, Coaching or Consulting, Website Design … there are dozens to choose from.)

These animated videos help "explain" what type or product or service you provide, and follow the typical "Hero's Journey" storyline of a character having a problem, meeting a guide or mentor (your product or service), solving the problem and then living happily ever after.

You simply fill in the text you want to display, choose a music track (if you want one) and the entire animated video is done. You can also add your own voice or other audio if you like.

To see some examples of videos I've made using it, go to https://ContentMarketingMachine.com/Bonus)

Save Time & Schedule

One of the biggest and best time-saving automation tools you'll come across is a social media scheduling app like Buffer or Hootsuite.

As I mentioned earlier, these tools allow you to pre-load and schedule status updates for virtually every social media network on the planet.

In addition, they also offer great analytics to measure your results, along with the ability to reshare or re-post popular content.

Automation = Awesome

There are more and more automation tools coming into the online marketplace all the time.

For a complete (and current) list of all my favorites, including training videos and demos, make sure you visit https://ContentMarketingMachine.com/Bonus)

Outsourcing is Key

Especially if you're a solopreneur, Business Coach, Consultant or one person shop, finding a virtual team to support your content marketing efforts is critical.

To really make your content machine hum, you'll want to find ways to outsource the more mundane elements of your work as much as possible.

Outside of creating the actual content itself, you can definitely outsource almost every other facet of the process.

For instance, say you record a 2-3 minute video on your iPhone sharing some great insights and strategies while you're on location at a conference.

Ideally, you can text or email that video file to your Virtual Assistant (VA) along with a suggested headline and 1-2 sentence summary description. He or she can then take the video and send it to SpeechPad or a similar service to get a written transcription and captions.

Once those come back, your VA can upload the video and its caption file (which was done for you by SpeechPad) to YouTube, Facebook, LinkedIn and other social media networks.

Next, your VA can send the written transcript of your 2-3 minute video (making it around 450-600 words long) along with the suggested title and summary description to a freelance writer and editor.

The writer and editor can edit and format the transcript so it's ready to publish as a written blog post, then send it back to your VA.

Next, your VA can publish the blog post on your website, LinkedIn and any other platforms, along with embedding the video of you sharing the strategy that was uploaded earlier on YouTube, Facebook, etc.

Then your VA can strip out the audio from your original video file and send it to a third party podcasting service. That service will edit and upload the audio for you as a new podcast episode, complete with the pre-made podcast intro and outro that you use on each episode.

Now your VA can have a freelance copywriter take the transcript and/or written blog post and create a marketing email to blast out to your list, linking back to the blog post, podcast episode or another place where you'll house the content online.

Finally, your VA can have the copywriter create some social media channel status updates built around the content, tweaking the language a bit for each specific platform, and including a stock image or related artwork to include as needed. Once that is done, your VA can copy and paste all the text into Buffer or another social media scheduling tool to share those status updates online at a pre-arranged date and time.

Really, with just your VA and some outside vendors (freelance writer and/or copywriter, third party podcast service, etc.) you've taken that 2-3 minute video and transformed it into several pieces of valuable content.

Best of all, you only spent the 2-3 minutes creating the content and then another few minutes coming up with the headline and summary, then sending your VA instructions on what to do with it.

Running all this through a project management software tool like Basecamp ensures everyone gets assigned his or her specific tasks, complete with due dates, detailed instructions, checkboxes and more.

Finding the right people to support your content marketing efforts can be a challenge. To find my favorite vendors, VAs and freelancers, visit https:// ContentMarketingMachine.com/Bonus to see who I use and recommend.

Outsource (or Else!)

There can be a real temptation to try and do everything by yourself when it comes to content marketing and promotion, but that would be a mistake. I speak from experience on this one, my friends!

You simply don't have enough hours in the day to do everything required, and, worse yet, you'll waste countless hours trying to navigate tech, tools and software instead of doing the one thing that matters most - creating awesome, unique and original content.

It can be tedious and time-consuming to put together a great team, but once you do, the amount of time, stress and frustration you'll save is well worth it.

Should You Hire Someone Else To Create Content For You?

I get asked this question a ton, and there are definitely some people who ascribe to the theory of having others create and publish content on their behalf.

I've even done this myself, having a freelance writer pen blog posts for me based around suggested headlines and guidelines I gave as an assignment inside Basecamp.

What I found, however, is that it's really, *really* hard for another person to capture *your* unique voice.

After all, the one thing you have that sets you apart from everyone else on this planet is your unique personality, communication style and *voice*. It's very hard for someone else to replicate that.

In reality, trying to outsource your voice is like trying to outsource parenting your kids - you might end up with a viable product, sure, but it won't be *your* unique product.

That's not to say it can't be done, but it's very, very difficult, and you need to find the right person and work with him or her closely to the point where he or she can finish your sentences for you.

Speak. Then Assign.

That's not to say you can't have a freelance writer take a transcript of you *talking* and turn it into an eBook or blog post. Since it's your "voice" down on the transcript, a writer will have a much easier time adhering to your style of communication - from the phrases and words you use to the stories you tell to the analogies you use to explain a strategy or technique.

Some people also hire a "co-host" to interview them for podcasts and videos, and that can work well too. As long as *you* are actively involved in creating the actual content that others consume, that is where the magic happens!

The Risk of ROI

Like a moth to the flame, many content marketers get sucked into the irresistible laser light show of fancy analytics, burning up valuable energy and patting themselves on the back for "measurables" that don't move the bottom line for your business.

I've said it before, and I'll say it again: *You cannot deposit likes, shares, video views or comments into your bank account.*

The best "ROI" you can ever hope for (and should be focused on!) is people giving you money for your product or service as a result of consuming your content.

As often as you can connect *that* type of activity to a specific piece of content, therein lies your biggest and best ROI.

Think of it this way: Paying customers and clients is like the golden center of a *Content Marketing ROI Circle.*

(I just made that term up, but it sounds official, right?)

Moving outward from the center of the circle (getting paid for your products and services), we find what I call "inbound" sales leads. These are people who initially came into your world via your content, and are now reaching out *directly* to ask how to go deeper in a particular area.

I love inbound leads who come in via your content, because these individuals are already warmed up and "pre-sold" on the value you can deliver. After all, your content has *already demonstrated* your authority and expertise, and it only makes logical sense to the person that working more closely with you in a paid engagement will generate even better results.

Typically, an inbound lead is reaching out to say, "I'm already sold ... just tell me how I can get my hands on it!"

Don't neglect or ignore the immense leverage your content creates with inbound sales leads. Unlike cold calls, you aren't starting from scratch in trying to get the other person to *know, like and trust* you. Your content has already done that.

At this point, it's more about knowing how to close a sale - how to position your offer and the unique and additional value it brings beyond what your content has already demonstrated.

(Note: To get my best advice on closing a sale, go to https:// ContentMarketingMachine.com)

Following Suit

Moving outward from paying clients and inbound leads, the next circle of ROI to expect with content marketing is what most networks call "Followers" - people who like your content enough that they want to be notified every time you publish something new.

Followers can either become invaluable prospects or remain time-sucking tire kickers.

Ultimately, if your content does its job, those people will either qualify or disqualify themselves over time.

The real metric here to watch is if your online "following" is growing on a particular social network or channel, that's a good thing and an indication that your content is resonating. Beyond that, don't get too concerned with follower counts.

Remember too, it's great if someone wants to follow you online, but the goal of your content is to always move them further toward the center of your content marketing circle. Stitching together pieces of similar content and creating sales funnels like we covered earlier is a great way to make that happen.

Engagement Matters

Moving outside of the "Follower" circle, you now get to the periphery of the content marketing circle.

Here we'll see what's typically referred to as "engagement" - post views, likes, shares, comments and so on.

While engagement is great, pay special attention to comments and shares. It's easy for anyone to view and hit "like" on one of your social media posts, for example. That's a pretty passive and simple action that almost anyone can take.

Taking the time to comment or share your content is a bigger step, one that means the person is much more *engaged* than someone who just viewed and/or liked your post.

Like anything else, you want to reply to every comment possible, utilizing that *context* (the person engaging with your content) to create a *conversation.* Take the chance to ask the person more about what he or she enjoyed or found valuable with your post, and when he or she tells you, ask him or her to take another step - subscribing to your podcast, leaving a review, signing up for a new eBook and so on.

Keep moving people further into your funnel - especially if they take the time to comment or share your stuff!

Other Metrics to Monitor

Especially with social media status updates, I'm always looking to see how many *clicks* I can generate. The more you can leverage social media networks to get people *off* that network and over to a landing page on your website, the better.

Focus on link clicks when measuring your content with a social media scheduling tool like Buffer or Hootsuite. Look for which types of content drive traffic over to your website, getting people to download your eBook, sign up for your webinar or whatever else it is you're asking the person to do.

As I mentioned before, you're always working on rented land with social media, so you'd be wise to move people *off* those networks and onto your email list, website or another digital "house" you own as soon as you can.

Tracking link clicks back to your landing pages for digital assets like an eBook or webinar registration is important ROI and something you should pay attention to.

One Final Warning About ROI

It's easy to *feel* like something is going to make a huge difference in the bottom line of your business.

I've had so many examples of this, from thinking that guest blogging for a certain publication or attending a certain mastermind event or getting an endorsement from an A-List person would revolutionize my business.

Today, I remove the emotional element and/or what people *say* will work and instead let the marketplace dictate the results.

For instance, did that guest post really send thousands of qualified visitors over to my landing page and generate hundreds of signups for my webinar? Even more, did all those people who registered end up purchasing my product or service after the webinar? Were they *qualified* leads? Or were they just tire kickers?

So many variables come into play when you're measuring ROI. At the end of the day, I *always* try and simplify to this one item: Did that piece of content or action I took end up resulting in people giving me money as a direct or indirect result?

What you find in today's online environment is so many people saying *their method* is the only surefire way to generate a certain result. For example, that Facebook Ads are the holy grail of webinar registrations. Or that LinkedIn is *the* place for B2B-related lead generation and client acquisition. (Wait - that one's implicity true!)

So many people are selling *their* story or *their* result, and in many instances *their* approach will work wonders for you too.

The only way to know for sure is to try it, and then (as I'll say until I'm blue in the face!) let the marketplace dictate the results.

Chapter 17:
Going Deeper - What To Do Next

There's no going back. If you aren't all-in on creating and leveraging your own unique, original content to sell your products and services, you're going to be all but invisible in today's marketplace.

The good news is, you have a proven strategy and system to follow. I've laid it out during this journey I've taken together, and I'm here to tell you that it works!

Best of all, *there are no more gatekeepers.*

I cannot stress enough how amazing and awesome this opportunity is.

The world I grew up in, huffing my way downtown to the Target Center basketball arena at age 16 for that high school sports writing contest, has moved on.

If, like me, you came of age during the 1980s and 1990s, before the Internet and social media became part of our daily lives, you know what a different world it was. You know how much harder it was to build and grow an audience of your own using content.

But the gatekeepers are gone, replaced by an online marketplace that gives everyone equal opportunity to *earn* the time, attention and interest of its various audiences.

Your *content* is that *currency*, the opportunity to "purchase" the type of lifestyle and business you've always dreamed of.

I've been doing it for almost a decade now, and it's only getting easier as the new technologies and tools coming into the marketplace make creating and publishing content faster and easier.

There's just one last, large impediment you must address before we finish our time together.

The #1 Obstacle to Massive Success

It's sinister, secretive and something none of us can escape.

Worst of all, it's an obstacle that you carry everywhere you go.

It's always talking, always chirping, always trying to hold you back.

Ready to hear what it is?

It's *you.*

It's the story you're telling yourself.

It's the lies you hear in your head that you act upon as if they're reality.

And, please know - I'm writing this as much for *me* as I am for you!

I struggle (often daily) with depression and negative self-talk.

Without turning this email into an episode of *Oprah* or *Dr. Phil,* I just want to be real with you.

I'm not immune to or above it, either.

So that's why, when I saw this quote today, I *knew* I needed to share it with you:

> **"Forces beyond your control can take away everything you possess except one thing, your freedom to choose how you will respond to the situation. You cannot control what happens to you in life, but you can always control what you will feel and do about what happens to you."**
> **- Man's Search for Meaning**

No matter how work (or life) punches you and me in the face, *we* get to decide how we react.

We get to decide what action we take in response to what our situation is or what happens to us.

Remember this: *Action destroys fear.*

This too: *Income improvement follows self-improvement.*

I don't know what state of mind you're in as you read this, but I want you to know two things: First, you're not alone. I'm in the trenches too, and I know countless others who are as well.

Second, you (and you alone) get to decide the meaning and impact you assign to what happens to you in work and life.

As I started this chapter, I had the familiar voices telling me I had nothing to say, nothing of value to add, no *content* that would make a real impact.

I had to ignore those voices, and then take *action* to destroy that fear.

Take Action, Always

The same is true for you, dear reader.

As you set out to create content that will entertain, inspire and engage your ideal audiences, remember that you (and only you!) can make it happen.

Nobody can replicate the secret sauce of your unique personality, life story and communication style.

Take your pain and turn it into purpose. Share the stories you've lived and the lessons you've learned, and show your ideal audience how it can help *them* achieve *their* goals as a result.

This book has given you what you need to begin the journey - the tools, tips and techniques that will ensure your content helps sell your products and services.

So it's time to stop reading and start *doing*.

Take action.

Punch fear in the face.

I believe in you and what you have to share.

More important, there are others out there who *need* to hear what you have to say.

Lastly, creating and sharing content like I've covered in these pages is the best way to monetize your knowledge, build your influence online and ensure you attract the type of paying clients and customers you'll love working with for years to come.

So go do it!

One More Thing

A master of content and presentations, the late Steve Jobs used to end his world-famous Apple keynotes with the phrase, "Oh yeah, I almost forgot ... there is one more thing."

The crowd would roar, knowing Jobs have saved his biggest (and best) surprise for last.

Allow me to share *one more thing* before we finish our time together.

I've got more. A *lot* more.

More content. More scripts. More tips. More templates.

I've got an exact, step-by-step walkthrough of how I've built my entire business over the past decade using content marketing.

I've also got the ability to *personally* create content for *you* and your business or brand.

It's all inside my online course, *Content Marketing Machine*.

If you've enjoyed this book (and I hope you have!), consider it a tasty appetizer to the companion online course.

You see, *Content Marketing Machine* is the steak dinner *and* dessert. In fact, it's me coming over to your house and cooking the entire meal for you!

Inside *Content Marketing Machine*, I share the exact, word-for-word, scripts I use to engage and sell to my ideal clients online, along with detailed sales funnel maps, email sequences, training videos, case studies and much more.

I show you *exactly* how my entire business works, pulling back the curtain and giving you the blueprint I follow when it comes to creating and utilizing content to sell your products and services. I also include 1-on-1 and group coaching, deeper dives on specific topics like email marketing, webinars and much more.

Finally, *Content Marketing Machine* also comes with the opportunity to have me *personally* write blog posts or create other types of content specifically for you and your business.

If you want to go deeper and see what *Content Marketing Machine* is all about, start with this free training session and webinar at <u>https://ContentMarketingMachine.com/Webinar</u>

Afterword

Whew!

What a ride we've been on.

I hope you feel inspired, excited and ready to take action by going out and creating some incredible content.

After all, this book will do you no good if you don't *apply* what you've discovered.

So get out and get after it!

Also, before I forget, can you do me a quick favor?

Tell me what you think of the book!

If you have a moment, please leave me an Amazon review. Go to https:// ContentMarketingMachine.com/Review and share your thoughts.

Book reviews are the oxygen this book needs to thrive on Amazon and other platforms, so please take a few moments to let others know what you think.

Leave your review here: https://ContentMarketingMachine.com/Review

I'd also love to hear from you personally!

You can email me anytime - john@linkedinriches.com

In addition, if you're a podcast fan, I've got a weekly online show called *Nemo Radio* where I share my latest tips and insights along with guest interviews featuring a virtual *who's-who* of marketing and business thought leaders.

Go to www.NemoRadio.com to subscribe and listen.

Lastly, if you want to know more about all the other tips, tools and resources I have available, head over to www.JohnNemo.net and have a look!

Once again: Thank you for sharing these pages with me, dear reader.

It's been so fun, and I have immense gratitude that you'd choose to spend your time sharing this journey with me.

See you on the Internet!

About the Author

As an author, speaker and online course creator, John Nemo helps individuals, organizations and businesses boost their brand, generate sales leads and increase revenue.

The son of two English teachers, John grew up in a home where the basement walls were lined floor-to-ceiling with books. A lifelong love of story led him to a career in journalism, where he started his career in 1997 as a reporter for *The Arizona Republic* and later the *Associated Press*.

John later worked in talk radio as a producer and on-air talent at *KTIS-AM* radio in Minneapolis-St. Paul. He also served as a freelance writer for hundreds of different magazines, newspapers and websites, covering topics ranging from Fantasy Football to Norwegian Architecture to Rock Music.

John has also worked as a national-award winning PR and Social Media Director for large trade associations in the debt collection and healthcare industries.

During its first 90 days, his 2009 PR campaign for the consumer financial education website *Ask Doctor Debt* led to more than 125 interviews across the

United States, reaching an estimated 25 million consumers and netting an estimated $1 million in free advertising/publicity value. John was also was able to secure a weekly, ongoing segment for *Ask Doctor Debt* and ACA International representatives on top-rated *Fox News Channel* that ran weekly for more than four months straight.

In 2010, John's PR campaign for the Minnesota Nurses Association (MNA) reached an estimated 133 million people in just 90 days and would have cost $5 million in advertising costs to duplicate. Billed as the largest nurses' strike in U.S. history, John's campaign garnered local, national and international media coverage from outlets as far away as *BBC Radio* in London.

During those same 90 days, John created and executed a Social Media Campaign for MNA that took its Facebook page from 0 to 11,000 fans, racking up 496,000 views. He also created and distributed content through an MNA Blog that generated 342,000 page views and 2,800 comments, along with building a YouTube channel that generated 97,000 views.

In the summer of 2011, John helped create and release the Minnesota Nurses Association iPhone/iPad App, which made MNA one of the first Labor Unions in the United States to release its own App. It allowed MNA's 20,000 members to get the latest association news, videos and updates, report unsafe staffing at their hospitals, look up and contact their local legislators and more.

In 2012, John Nemo left MNA to start his own marketing agency, Nemo Media Group, which provided services including Consulting, Website Design, Copywriting, Video Marketing, Social Media Marketing, Content Creation, Sales Presentations and more for clients across the United States.

In 2014, John created his first online course, *LinkedIn Riches,* followed by *Webinars That Work* and *Content Marketing Machine.* Learn more about John's online courses and coaching programs at www.JohnNemo.net.

15098677R00123

Printed in Great Britain
by Amazon